Foreword by

THE WAY OF THE DRAGON SLAYER

7 REASONS MEN NEED BROTHERS

DANNY SILK

Scripture taken from the New King James Version. Copyright © 1982 by Thomas Nelson, Inc. Used by permission. All rights reserved.

Scripture quotations marked "ESV" are taken from The Holy Bible, English Standard Version. Copyright © 2000; 2001 by Crossway Bibles, a division of Good News Publishers. Used by permission. All rights reserved.

Scripture quotations from THE MESSAGE. Copyright © by Eugene H. Peterson 1993, 1994, 1995, 1996, 2000, 2001, 2002. Used by permission of NavPress Publishing Group.

Scripture quotations marked "NIV" are taken from the Holy Bible, New International Version®. NIV®. Copyright © 1973, 1978, 1984 by International Bible Society. Used by permission of Zondervan. All rights reserved.

Scripture quotations marked (NLT) are taken from the Holy Bible, New Living Translation, copyright © 1996. Used by permission of Tyndale House Publishers, Inc., Wheaton, IL 60189 USA. All rights reserved.

Scripture quotations marked "AMP" are taken from The Amplified Bible, Old Testament. Copyright © 1965, 1987, by the Zondervan Corporation. Used by permission. All rights reserved.

Scripture quotations marked TPT are from The Passion Translation®. Copyright © 2017, 2018, 2020 by Passion & Fire Ministries, Inc. Used by permission. All rights reserved. ThePassionTranslation.com.

Designer: Anditya Dita

CONTENTS

Acknowledgments v
Foreword vii

Chapter 1: Here Be Dragons 1
Chapter 2: Man with God 25
    The Nature of the Dragon: The Fear of Judgment,
    Punishment, and Unworthiness 31
    Riding the Dragon: Trying to Play God 35
    Facing the Dragon: Unraveling
    the Punishment Paradigm 39
    The Way of the Dragon Slayer: Discipline and Dreams 45

Chapter 3: Man with Himself 57
    The Nature of the Dragon: The Fear of Inadequacy,
    Self-Hatred, and Disqualification 63
    Riding the Dragon: Projection, Isolation,
    and Self-Medication 67
    Facing the Dragon: Remember Who You Are 73
    The Way of the Dragon Slayer: Knowing Yourself 81

Chapter 4: Man with Woman 91
    The Nature of the Dragon: The Fear of Rejection,
    Disconnection, and Betrayal 97
    Riding the Dragon: Subtle Predators 101
    Facing the Dragon: The Sexy Butler 107
    The Way of the Dragon Slayer: Learning Her Needs 111

Chapter 5: Man with Man 127
    The Nature of the Dragon: The Fear of Competition,
    Covenant, and Sacrifice 135
    Riding the Dragon: Men Who Won't Commit 139

    Facing the Dragon: Jonathan, David,
        and a Band of Mighty Men 145

    The Way of the Dragon Slayer:
        Building Covenant Friendships 151

Chapter 6: Man with Nature 163

    The Nature of the Dragon: The Fear of Insignificance,
        Vulnerability, and Eternity 169

    Riding the Dragon: Hard Hearts 175

    Facing the Dragon: But Did You Die? 183

    The Way of the Dragon Slayer: Seasoned Courage 189

Chapter 7: Man and Machine 203

    The Nature of the Dragon: The Fear of Failure,
        Being Out of Control, and Death 207

    Riding the Dragon: Who's in Control? 211

    Facing the Dragon: Control Your Freaking Self 217

    The Way of the Dragon Slayer: Learn from the Masters 223

Chapter 8: Man and Provision 235

    The Nature of the Dragon: The Fear of Lack,
        Limitation, and Comparison 243

    Riding the Dragon: Who Benefits? 247

    Facing the Dragon: Upgrading Our Vision 253

    The Way of the Dragon Slayer: Building Your Legacy 259

Chapter 9: Billy's Twelve 271

ACKNOWLEDGMENTS

Sheri Silk - You've required the best that was in me to show up and become your leader. I don't know who else on earth could've done it! I love you with all my heart, choose you every day and cannot wait to see how this wonderful story unfolds together with you.

Allison Armerding Slack - These books don't happen without your genius giftedness applied! I am forever in your debt for your brilliant assembly, contributions and skill helping me get so many thoughts into 'read-speak'. Thanks again for all your support!

My "OG's": (Original Guys) - Ben, Bob, Christian, Craig, Eric, Shain, Wes, Jon, Joe, Ron, Charles, & Allen, you've all had such a great influence and effect on me. I have great respect for how each of you have sown your talents and reaped the kingdom's rewards. I am inspired to continue on with each of you in this journey and cannot thank you enough for your brotherhood!

The Men of Mountain Chapel - Bill Johnson, Kris Vallotton, Bill Derryberry, Jerry Kloose, Buck Steele, Charlie Harper, Barry Leeder, and others, you shaped me as a man of God. When I had nowhere else to look, you showed me what connector, provider, protector looked like. My legacy thanks you all!

To future Dragon Slayers - This book, gathering model, and movement belongs to you! Run with this until the end of mankind. I thank all the serious "Original Gatherers" who start a tree of downline momentum with fruit that lasts. I appreciate your faithful stewardship of the call of God on your lives. Thank you for adding your strength!

FOREWORD

Jesus was known in His community as "the carpenter" (Mark 6:3).

In Matthew's Gospel, He is also called "the carpenter's son" (Matthew 13:55).

We postmodern men miss the ancient power of the connection; we have nothing in our experience to help us grasp the rugged force of these titles. Carpenter, carpenter's son. Hours upon hours, months upon years in a real workshop, with real wood and sharp tools, older hand upon young hand, learning by guided instruction. Being fathered.

Because within that loving framework there was wisdom and counsel being passed on, too.

"I met a girl today." "Did you? Tell me about her."

"I saw two boys in a fight today." "And what was it like?"

For millennia, human cultures all around the world understood that boys do not become men simply by getting older. They must be shown the way; they must be initiated into manhood by older men. Even Jesus of Nazareth took this journey.

Oh, how the soul of man still yearns for this. These days, if a man needs to learn something he doesn't understand, he searches YouTube. It's not exactly an initiation. Not even close. The entire experience of "YouTube mentoring" leaves a massive hole in a man's heart, because it offers merely facts (often conflicting facts) and nothing of what Joseph offered Jesus in his woodshop, what boys had in abundance through every century of human experience prior to this one.

I grew up in an alcoholic home. My dad failed to teach me anything about women, money, careers, the world, or God. But my grandfather—his father—took me under his wing and during summers on his cattle ranch I learned to use a tractor, saddle a horse, fix irrigation, drive a pickup, and a host of other wonderful lessons. But the greater gift by far, he offered me the fundamental food of the masculine soul—he gave me initiation, that time-honored tradition of masculine formation under the care of an older man. When I returned home each fall, back to the suburbs and strip malls of Los Angeles, it was like returning from another planet. For even in the '60s, American culture had long abandoned masculine initiation.

That was ages ago. Since then, the bottom fell out. All we offer boys and men-who-are-still-mostly-boy-inside nowadays are cell phones, internet porn, Google, and YouTube for all other questions.

Danny Silk and his community are trying to rectify that. He is offering a path of masculine initiation, offered by men to men. A very loving thing to do. And very needed.

In the following pages you will discover how men have thought about the core issues of life and better still, how they have faced them since time immemorial. It's a treasure-trove of masculine wisdom and encouragement. But I need to warn you: Danny doesn't mince words. He says some controversial things and he says them boldly. If you want someone to shoot straight with you about the masculine crisis in our culture and in our souls, you will enjoy this book immensely. More importantly, if you want an older man in a fellowship of men offering you timeless wisdom, you will love this book.

But it's not YouTube, and Danny isn't going to coddle you the way postmodern culture does. He understands the dragons you face, and he understands that soft men and soft advice slay no dragons. If you want victories, if you want to become a solid man with fire in your belly, read on. Better still, get a couple guys around you and read it together. The world may be collapsing but God is raising up good men to raise up good men. It is one of the great God movements of our time, and you can be a part of it.

John Eldredge
Colorado 2024

CHAPTER 1
HERE BE DRAGONS

In the second book in J. R. R. Tolkein's *The Lord of the Rings* trilogy, *The Two Towers*, we encounter the kingdom of Rohan, realm of the horse lords, a people with a noble history and warrior culture. Tragically, Rohan has become almost totally undefended and is on the brink of collapse because its king, Théoden, is captive to an evil wizard who has been weaving a plan to invade Rohan with his armies. This wizard has successfully hypnotized the king and bound his will through lies, convincing him that the growing threat of the enemy is not his concern, and he would be better taking a powerless and self-protective stance of non-involvement. Under this spell, Théoden has been robbed of his strength and, though still middle-aged, now appears decrepit, blind, and a hundred years old, practically on the verge of death.

In a climactic scene, the good wizard, Gandalf, enters King Théoden's hall and breaks the enchantment under which he has been languishing. The king wakes from his stupor and the years fall away from him. He rises from his throne as he truly is, a king with much strength and courage left to lead his people. Taking his rightful place as a warrior king, he rallies his armies to face the enemy in two great battles before he is fatally injured. As his life ebbs away, his face shows nothing but peace. "I go now to my fathers," he says, "in whose mighty company I shall now not be ashamed."

Like King Théoden, the men of the West today have fallen under an enchantment that has rendered them mentally and spiritually weakened and all but overthrown. They have allowed themselves to be lulled into captivity to entertainment, pornography, and material comforts while simultaneously being bullied and brainwashed into thinking that their masculine virtues are no longer needed, or worse, "toxic." Today's culture has made the "patriarchy" the scapegoat for social ills and demanded that men surrender their power as well as the responsibilities that come with it, insisting that we no longer need men to fill their traditional roles. Since this view became dominant in the 1960s, we have seen nearly three generations of men grow up struggling to find their way in the world, and the result has been catastrophic. Without men fulfilling their traditional roles and responsibilities—not only in the home but in every social institution—our once-strong culture has degenerated into a painful landscape of broken marriages, fatherlessness, addiction, crime, mental illness, corruption, abuse, slavery, and child sacrifice (literally—we just typically kill the children before they're born). Meanwhile, the enemies of Western liberal democracy, Judeo-Christian civilization, and ultimately, humanity, are positioning themselves to grow ever more powerful as we grow weaker, and ultimately to take possession of all that is ours.

But hope is not lost. One by one, men are starting to awaken to the reality that we are, in fact, in a spiritual war, that the enemy has been advancing while we've been in this enchanted stupor, and that the lies we've believed about God, ourselves, our families, and society are simply not true. Men are not superfluous or toxic. We are necessary. The future of civilization and humanity are at stake, and we have a critical and heroic role to play in pushing back the advancing darkness and destruction.

The Deconstructive Experiment

How did we end up here? Some label it "progress," but it's more accurate to say that men in the West are currently enmeshed in a massive experiment of cultural deconstruction. Specifically, we have been deconstructing three cornerstones of wisdom that have held up what "manhood" means throughout human history and certainly since the dawn of Judeo-Christian civilization.

First, we have deconstructed traditional male gender roles. Contrary to what we often hear these days, traditional masculine roles are not arbitrary or "socially constructed." In fact, they stretch across cultures back through human history. In *Manhood in the Making*, anthropologist David D. Gilmore makes the case that the "deep structure" of manhood across cultures arises not just from male biology or psychology but from how society and culture interact with these things and set expectations for the proper role men are needed to play. If we think of culture as the story humans are telling about what is important to them and prescribing behavior around that, then manhood is what men are supposed to do and how they're supposed to do it in that story.

In every human culture up to the present, men have a three-part role that is unavoidably rooted in the design of the family, which is to *procreate* children, *provide* for their family, and *protect* their family. These roles also extend out into the wider community, because culture has alway recognized the family as the fundamental unit of society. All traditional morality—honor, courage, trustworthiness, sexual fidelity, etc.—is built around the standards and obligations that these primary relationships require.

But of course, the second thing we've been deconstructing is the foundation of our morality in Judeo-Christian culture, namely the Bible. Scripture not only affirms the three traditional family-based male roles but specifically reveals how they are grounded in the greater divine purpose for the human family that God has been unfolding since Creation. Genesis 1 and 2 describe how God created humans in God's image and gave them what Bible scholars call the Cultural Mandate:

> Then God said, "Let Us make man in Our image, according to Our likeness; let them have dominion over the fish of the sea, over the birds of the air, and over the cattle, over all the earth and over every

> creeping thing that creeps on the earth." So God created man in His [own] image; in the image of God He created him; male and female He created them. Then God blessed them, and God said to them, "Be fruitful and multiply; fill the earth and subdue it; have dominion over the fish of the sea, over the birds of the air, and over every living thing that moves on the earth." (Genesis 1:26-28)

In the Genesis account, the man was specifically charged with "tending" (Heb. *'ābad,* which means to "work" and "serve") and "keeping" (Heb. *šāmar,* which means to "guard," "preserve," and "keep watch over") the garden. The man is also the one who "shall leave his father and mother and be joined to his wife, and they shall become one flesh" (Gen 2:24)—in other words, he was supposed to initiate marriage and the formation of a new family. According to Scripture, the procreator, protector, and provider roles were all part of man's design from the beginning and were directed at a purpose far higher than mere survival. Men were to cultivate an entire planet and make it part of the garden of God, a home where the human family could live and thrive.

These roles and their purpose didn't disappear when man sinned, either. From Genesis 3 on, the rest of the Bible shows how sin caused men to violate and abuse their roles, but also that God always had a strategic plan to restore us through the death of His Son. The beauty and power of the gospel is not merely that we can go to heaven when we die, it's that through being reconciled to the Father, we can be restored to our original design and fulfill our roles in ways that bring life and flourishing as God intended, rather than remaining under the curse. The fact that there is no longer "male nor female" in Christ doesn't mean Jesus deconstructed gender roles. It means we all have access to the Father, and thus have hope to become true men and true women, the best version of ourselves.

Yet as we have deconstructed the Bible and Christianity, we have removed the ideal moral vision for men to serve in traditional roles in a Christlike way. And with the help of widely available birth control, abortion, and relaxed divorce laws, we've done our best to separate what used to be united in one reality—sex, marriage, and making babies—so that men can supposedly be free from many of the consequences of violating the old moral codes. In the process, we've deconstructed the family and removed it as the highest achievement and responsibility in a man's life.

Thirdly, as a consequence of deconstructing male roles and their divine meaning and purpose, we've also deconstructed the cultural pathways by which we help boys become men. Another universal aspect of the "deep structure" of manhood across human cultures, states Gilmore, is the understanding that manhood "is not a natural condition but rather a precarious or artificial state that boys must win against powerful odds. This recurrent notion that manhood is problematic, a critical threshold that boys must pass through testing, is found at all levels of sociocultural development regardless of what other alternative roles are recognized."[1]

Boys are different from girls in this respect. No one tells a girl to "be a woman" like we tell a boy to "be a man." Gilmore's theory is that this is because the psychosocial task of leaving boyhood requires a young man to change his relationship with his mother in a way that girls don't experience:

> To become a separate person the boy must perform a great deed. He must pass a test; he must break the chain to his mother. He must renounce his bond to her and seek his own way in the world. His masculinity thus represents his separation from his mother and his entry into a new and independent social status recognized as distinct and opposite from hers. In this view the . . . principal

---

1 | David D. Gilmore, *Manhood in the Making: Culture Concepts of Masculinity*, (Yale University, 1990) 11.

> danger to the boy is not a unidimensional fear of the punishing father but a more ambivalent fantasy-fear about the mother . . . In sum, manhood imagery can be interpreted from this post-Freudian perspective as a defense against the eternal child within, against puerility, against what is sometimes called the Peter Pan complex.[2]

The "great deed" a boy must perform to prove and gain manhood may differ in details across cultures, but in general it requires him to demonstrate courage in all its forms—a willingness to endure pain, face danger, and perform acts of strength and prowess. He must confront his fear and weakness and overcome his desire for comfort. And he must also do this in public where he can be seen and measured by other men. Without this, he cannot grow up.

Not only has Western culture stopped requiring displays of courage, endurance, and resilience from boys—we have actively encouraged boys to stay boys by providing them with whatever they need to avoid facing their fears and to stay addicted to ease and comfort. Physically, our young men have become unhealthy and unfit—due to obesity and lack of fitness, only two out of five between the ages of seventeen and twenty-four would qualify for service in the military.[3] The vast majority of boys are exposed to digital pornography by the age of eight, and studies show that many become addicted, which actively inhibits the development of their attraction to real women and the social skills required of a relationship with one. Marriage rates have been dropping as many young men don't feel marriageable and others have become convinced that the risks of marriage—being controlled by a woman, or financially ruined through divorce—outweigh the rewards.

---

2 | Gilmore, *Manhood in the Making*, 28-29.

3 | https://www.cdc.gov/physicalactivity/resources/unfit-to-serve/index.html

For decades, the number of young men in the workforce has been declining, and today a third of twenty-five-year-old men in the United States don't have a full-time job. Most of these young men opting out of work don't have college degrees and feel discouraged about their salary prospects, social status, and marriageability, seeing that real earnings for men without degrees in our society have dropped thirty percent over the last few decades.[4] Young men also spend an average of seven hours a day doing leisure activities like playing video games and many more are living at home with their parents, meaning they are being taken care of rather than stepping into the responsibility of taking care of a family of their own.[5] Young men who do go to college now enter an environment where students are encouraged to avoid mental, emotional, and relational risk-taking and retreat to "safe spaces" where their beliefs will not be challenged and they can indulge their feelings however they want. As Greg Lukianoff and Jonathan Haidt explain in *The Coddling of the American Mind*, "safetyism"—the belief that we ought to protect kids from all harm because "what doesn't kill you makes you weaker"—has spread through parenting culture, university life, and now all aspects of American culture, producing kids who are actually more anxious, depressed, suicidal, and lacking in mental and emotional coping skills for life.[6] If we could imagine a culture that was intentionally designed to produce a generation of Peter Pans and Lost Boys, we probably couldn't do much better than what we're doing right now.

---

4 | Jacob Zinkula and Jason Lalljee, "Young men aren't working as much as they used to — and they have less financial freedom than previous generations," *Business Insider*, June 3, 2023, https://www.businessinsider.com/young-men-work-less-financially-independent-salary-marriageability-2023-6?op=1

5 | Tony Dokoupil and Martin Finn, "Millions of men have dropped out of the workforce, leaving companies struggling to fill jobs: It's a matter of our national identity,'" *CBS News*, January 26, 2023. https://www.cbsnews.com/news/men-workforce-work-companies-struggle-fill-jobs-manufacturing/

6 | Greg Lukianoff and Jonathan Haidt, *The Coddling of the American Mind*, (New York, NY: Penguin Books, 2018).

Strong Men vs. Weak Men

It turns out that cultural deconstruction means cultural *destruction*. Progressive ideology has failed to produce an alternative way for men to be men, and our whole society is feeling the loss of our protectors, providers, and procreators. Worse, things will only continue to decline until real men show up to stop it—men who cling to the ancient wisdom of manly roles, their grounding in the Bible, and the necessity of courage, endurance, and resilience. The question is, where are these real men going to come from?

Somewhere in the current age of "memes," I ran across a saying that I've used numerous times speaking to men:

> Hard times create strong men
> Strong men create good times
> Good times create weak men
> Weak men create hard times

This cycle reminds me of the principle of momentum. One of my childhood friends had an above-ground pool in his backyard. We spent many an afternoon in that pool, and one of our favorite activities was making a whirlpool. We would start walking around the outer edge of the pool wall in the same direction, and after a while of concerted effort, the water would start moving with us. We then started to run as fast as we could to speed up our water vortex, and eventually, we had enough momentum that we could start to lift our feet and ride on the current we had created. We only needed to add a few occasional pushes to keep things moving. If someone joined us in the pool, they would be swept along without being required to exert the same force we had to create the whirlpool, but we knew we had to tell them to "push" with us to keep it going.

Cultural momentum is a beautiful thing—generations of strong men work hard and sacrifice to create good times, and their children and grandchildren get to enjoy the fruits of their labor. The danger is that unless we teach these generations to appreciate the sacrifices of the strong men who came before and follow in their footsteps by "pushing" to create and preserve good times of their own, then the descendents of the strong men become weak men. Weak men are selfish consumers. Like the prodigal son in the parable, they take their father's inheritance and squander it, ultimately leaving them lost, poor, and humiliated. They can repent and be forgiven and restored, but the only way they will be able to leave an inheritance for their children is if they choose to become strong and begin to work and sacrifice. More likely, their children will have to endure hard times that they themselves never did, and these children must allow the hard times to make them strong.

One question for us is, where are we in this cycle? If we look closer, the reality is a bit more complex. There are still some strong men out there creating good times for their families, communities, nations, and the world. There are a lot of weak men exploiting the benefits of these good times to indulge their own pleasures and avoid responsibility. But there is also a minority of evil men actively and strategically working to destroy the "strong men" momentum they've inherited and reverse it—to dismantle the culture that honors the roles of provider, protector, and procreator, and promote an anti-culture that encourages men to reject these roles. One sign that they are succeeding is how quickly and easily children raised in traditional, intact families—either homegrown in America or immigrants from other traditional cultures—can become seduced by this culture of deconstruction. The cultural momentum has shifted. Hard times have begun and will get harder, and there will only be a reversal of momentum because strong men begin to rise up to push against the tide.

I believe this is the moment we are in—a moment where men must rise and become strong enough to resist the culture coming at us and work to restore and preserve the ancient ruins of manhood for the next generation. The first challenge—resisting the culture—is the hardest, because it requires the most courage to shift out of comfort and inertia and begin to confront the forces lulling us to sleep as they carry us to our destruction.

In this regard, some men today are like the Hobbits at the beginning of

The Lord of the Rings, blissfully living in one of the only remaining bubbles of "normal" left in the West, unaware of encroaching evil or of the protectors who have kept them safe for generations. These men have benefited from their family, community, and cultural inheritance and been able to grow up, get a job, get married, and have a family without an inordinate amount of struggle. They assume the institutions that were there for them growing up—church, school, public safety, etc.—are still there to help raise and support their kids, only to be blindsided when their children announce that they are leaving the church or confused about their gender. This is what happens when we forget that evil exists and it's our job to deal with it. Similarly when Frodo and his friends learn of the Ring and the rise of the dark lord Sauron, they struggle to believe first that their beautiful Shire is in real danger, and then that they, small as they are, can do anything to stop it. A beautiful place is terrible to leave, but they finally realize this is what they must do if there's any hope of preserving that beautiful place.

Other men will only resist the culture if, like King Théoden, they experience a spiritual awakening and deliverance from the deception to which they have succumbed. The lie that has entrapped a generation of men—that they can still live a meaningful life while staying in control, avoiding all struggle, responsibility, or commitments, and surrounding themselves with pleasure and comfort—is incredibly seductive. It's the fantasy of every little boy who doesn't want to grow up. But at some point they must see this lie for what it is. The things they've been avoiding—pain, sacrifice, self-discipline, work, covenant—are actually the only things that will transform them into a true man who can live a truly meaningful life, while staying addicted to comfort and control will only destroy his future. I think Elon Musk framed this perfectly: "Comfort is a drug. Give a weak man regular sex, good food, and cheap entertainment and he'll throw his ambitions right out the window. Comfort is where dreams go to die."

Seeing the threat of evil for what it is, and seeing through the lies for what they are, is where the journey for our desperately needed strong men begins. This is where we hear the call to courage, adventure, and great deeds. The next step is clarifying how to answer that call.

Facing the Dragons

Makers of old maps sometimes drew sea monsters or serpentine creatures in unexplored territories. An inscription on a 16th-century globe had a stamp on these uncharted voids that read: "Here Be Dragons!" Real or imaginary, dragons have always represented that which men have yet to face and conquer, and therefore, that which they fear. The question every man must answer to become a man is, "What am I going to do about my fear?"

I have heard the word "fear" defined by the acronym "False Evidence Appearing Real." Wherever fear is present, there are most likely lies, deception, and distortion involved at some level. When we are in fear, we do not fully perceive reality as it is—particularly the reality of who we are, why we are here, and who God is for us. And we will respond to FEAR in one of two ways:

> Forget Everything And Run
> OR
> Face Everything And Rise

One of the classic stories where we see the deceptive nature of fear and these two responses play out is the account of Moses sending the twelve spies to scout out the Promised Land. When they return and give their report, they all agree about the facts—the land is rich and fruitful, and it's full of giants and walled cities. They are completely divided, however, on how to respond to these facts. Caleb and Joshua say, "Let's go take the land now. We've got this." They are ready to face everything and rise! But the other ten guys say, "No way! Did we mention the giants?" It's not long before these ten fear-mongers have spread their view of the situation throughout the entire community, and within a day, the Israelites are talking about ditching Moses, appointing a new leader, and heading back to Egypt. They all agree—forget everything and run!

Now, I'm sure if you or I stumbled across the path of a giant, our self-preservation instinct would probably kick in just as if we had encountered a bear, a lion . . . or a dragon. The urge to run away would be powerful. The problem was that God had given Israel an assignment to go take the land. This is why Caleb and Joshua urged them, "Only do not rebel against the LORD, nor fear the people of the land, for they [are] our bread; their protection has departed from them, and the LORD [is] with us. *Do not fear them*" (Numbers 14:9). In their case, running away wouldn't have been simply giving into a natural urge, it would have been outright rebellion. It would have been stepping out from under God's authority and obeying another voice and influence. Caleb and Joshua understood the assignment and how authority worked, and this defined their perception of who they were, what they were capable of, and who God was for them. They refused to let fear of anything else displace their fear of God, and as a result, they knew they had the full backing of the kingdom of heaven to fulfill their assignment. The giants didn't have the power to defy God.

As the rest of the story plays out, we see the extreme consequences that come from these two opposite reactions to fear. Thanks to their rebellion, that entire generation of Israelites were forbidden from entering the Promised Land and died in the wilderness. Joshua and Caleb were the two exceptions, and they not only survived but led the next generation to conquer the land. Caleb specifically asked to take one of the giant strongholds as his own inheritance (Joshua 14:6-15). He never lost sight of his assignment—forty years in the wilderness were just more time to train and prepare to get it done.

Joshua and Caleb said, "The giants are our bread." My friend Kris Vallotton often says, "The Dogs of Doom stand at the Door of Destiny." And Carl Jung put it directly: "Where your fear is, there is your task." It's not hard to find the "great deeds" or tests that will enable us to transform from boys to men. We just need to do the things we're afraid of. On one level, these things will be unique to us and the particulars of our story. But on a deeper level, the fears we face as men are very similar. I call them the Seven Dragons:

1. Man with God: The fear of punishment, judgment, and unworthiness
2. Man with Himself: The fear of inadequacy, self-hatred, and disqualification
3. Man with Women: The fear of rejection, disconnection, and betrayal
4. Man with Men: The fear of competition, covenant, and sacrifice
5. Man with Nature: The fear of insignificance, vulnerability, and eternity
6. Man with Machine: The fear of failure, being out of control, and death
7. Man with Provision: The fear of lack, limitation, and comparison

Each of the relationships on the left represents a critical area of our assignment as men—an assignment that, once again, isn't arbitrary or socially constructed but divinely designed and authorized by God for us to fulfill. We have specific responsibilities there as providers, protectors, and procreators—or, in my preferred term, *connectors*. The procreative role of a man is not just to beget children, but to initiate and form the connections with his wife and children that establish them as his family, to name them and give them a sense of identity, belonging, vision, and mission. This is just as critical as protecting them and providing for them.

On the right are the classic fears and insecurities men experience around these relationships and responsibilities. These are the dragons every man must slay if he hopes to rise and become the man he was created and called to be. As men we must understand that the strength of our character is obtained through building our courage to deal with our weakness. Bravery comes from being brave! An old Native American proverb says, "A brave man dies but once, a coward many times." It is through facing our dragons that we prove our entire life as a man is about overcoming through our partnership with Jesus, the ultimate Dragon Slayer!

Fear, Love, and Brotherhood

My plan in this book is to tackle each of these seven dragons in turn, looking at how they manifest in our lives, how to face them, and what happens when we do. My hope is that in describing and illustrating them in detail, you will recognize where they have shown up in your own story, where you are in the process of learning to resist the internal and external momentum urging you to run away from them, and what you need to do to begin to confront them head-on like a man.

As we journey together through the land of the dragons, over and over we will see three primary themes emerge, which are critical to understand if we hope to become dragon slayers.

The first theme is that we must learn to see through the distortion of fear so that we can identify the dragons for what they are. God, ourselves, women, other men, nature, machines, and provision are not actually dragons—they are, in fact, the precious things we ought to love, work, live, and die for. But fear makes these relationships and responsibilities *look* like dragons, causing them to trigger our ego and instinct for self-preservation. It is this survivalist, self-preservationist instinct in us that we must master to slay the dragons of our fears.

This instinct runs incredibly deep in us, because we live in a world full of pain and danger, and our brains are designed to triage threats in our environment and prime our bodies to react to them. However, our ability to perceive threats accurately and react to them effectively is not automatic. These are skills that we must develop, mature, and hone. Without training and successful recovery after bad experiences, our ability to discern true threats from false threats will be unreliable, and our reactions will remain at the primitive levels of fight, flight, or freeze. This is why many men end up attacking or running away from the most important people or opportunities in their lives—they have never dealt with the wounding, trauma, and poor coping skills that began in childhood.

Facing the dragons requires us to look inward and unravel the distorted core beliefs driving our fear, replacing them with God's truth. This is how we become masters of ourselves. The self-preservationist in us is always looking to control externals to maintain his sense of comfort and safety. The true man learns to control himself and endure discomfort to fulfill his responsibilities. This is how he stops wasting his strength and starts channeling it to build virtue, which is true power.

The second theme is the *why* that must consume us if we are to become dragon slayers. The self-preservationist in us is driven by fear. The mature man we are called to become is driven by that which casts out fear—love (1 John 4:18). Love orients us to put others before ourselves—to want what is best for them and to sacrificially offer our strength and resources for their benefit. When love is the animating force behind us playing our roles as providers, protectors, and connectors, we become the best version of ourselves, the men the world needs. Only men with mature love have the power to stop the deconstruction ravaging our homes, communities, and nations, and restore the ancient paths of wisdom that enable not only men, but all people and especially the most vulnerable, to thrive.

The third theme is the consequence of the previous two, and that is that men can only become true men *together*. Other men induct men into manhood. Fathers play a huge role in this. The epidemic of fatherlessness in American society is one of the most obvious signs of men opting out of their roles and responsibilities as providers, protectors, and connectors. The negative effects this fatherless epidemic has produced in the lives of each of the last few generations are absolutely devastating—it's correlated with almost every bad outcome in life, from crime to incarceration, addiction, teenage pregnancy, suicide, gender confusion, lower income, poor education, and struggles in marriage, career, health, and more. Kids—boys and girls—need their dads. Boys especially need father figures to show them what true manhood looks like and how to become a man.

But once initiated, young men cannot advance and mature in manhood without brothers to encourage, challenge, and fight alongside them. True manhood is a brotherhood that holds men accountable to keep being men—to stay courageous, to choose virtue, to show up and do the hard work to face your fears and fulfill your responsibilities. But in our comfortable, self-indulgent, disconnected culture, men have become isolated from each other in an unprecedented way, and we are not better for it. This generation of Peter Pans and Lost Boys in adult bodies exists because we have given them the permission and means to hide behind their computer screens and social media façades, playing games, consuming porn, taking shots as armchair critics online, and finding false communities of overgrown boys who affirm this selfish lifestyle, without ever being confronted and called out on how unmanly they are being. As Proverbs 18:1 says, "A man who isolates himself seeks his own desire; He rages against all wise judgment." This is actual toxic masculinity—a culture that allows men to stay isolated and immature, and thus encourages them to become unavailable predatory consumers instead of connected, protective providers.

Over the years, my friendships with other men have brought great strength, accountability, and challenge into my life. These men have inspired me with their example, believed in me more than I have in myself, called me on my selfishness and cowardice at times, and consistently sharpened me to be a better man, just as Proverbs 27:17 says, "As iron sharpens iron, So a man sharpens the countenance of his friend." Most of these men I connected with serving in the trenches of church leadership. But a few years ago, something happened that inspired me to be more intentional about cultivating a "band of brothers" in my life.

On a drizzly day in the Portland, Oregon area, my friend Bob Hasson and I spent the day with Wm. Paul Young, who authored the best-selling book *The Shack*. We talked all day and went to several of Paul's favorite sites and places to eat. He shared many stories that day, but for me one stood out above them all. He told us of a friend of his who had recently spent some time with Billy Graham. Billy was in his early nineties at the time of this visit. Paul's friend asked Billy what, if anything, he would change if he had it all to do over again. His answer to this question sent me on a journey that impacts the way I live life. Billy said that he wouldn't have only done the broadcasts, conferences, or campaigns—he would have also gathered twelve men and poured his life into them.

At the time I heard this story, I was traveling 220 days a year doing conferences. I was immediately convicted that while my life felt busy and productive for the kingdom, I was missing this crucial piece for achieving true impact. After all, I knew another guy who had done exactly what Billy had described, and was still changing the world—Jesus Christ. If each of His twelve disciples had followed His example and made twelve more disciples, and they had continued with this model, it wasn't surprising that within two hundred years, Christianity had spread throughout the Roman empire. Surely the same method could reconstruct a culture of healthy manhood with the momentum to turn the tide of deconstruction.

Soon after hearing this story, I began choosing the twelve men I wanted to run with for the next few decades, and christened the group "Dragon Slayers." We agreed that our mission was to be "a band of brothers who raise up an army of fathers to heal a generation of orphaned sons." This is our high calling as men and we believe that restoration of brotherhood is the vehicle of that healing. We also formulated a creed expressing the standard of manhood we were committing to honor together:

DRAGON SLAYERS CREED

Men always protect
They never exploit the weak

Men always set the standard of love
They never hate their enemy

Men always provide resources, strength, and identity
They never consume or compromise the quality of life for others

Men always control themselves from the inside out
They never control other people

Men take full responsibility
They never blame others or neglect their responsibilities

Men sacrifice for the benefit of others
They never sacrifice others for their own benefit

Men live submitted to other men
They never live as the masters of their own universe

In the coming chapters, you'll meet many of these Dragon Slayers and hear stories from their own journeys of learning to face their fears, embrace their manly roles and responsibilities out of love, and grow as men through the sharpening presence of brothers in their lives. These are ordinary men who are, I believe, changing the world as they simply choose to be the men they were created to be in their vital relationships. If they can get up and "slay every day," then you can too!

> And so, as God said to Job, I call you to "Prepare yourself like a man" (Job 38:3 NIV)! It's time to wake up, shake off the fog that has settled on you as you have succumbed to forces lulling you into inaction and disengagement, and brace yourself for adventure. The dragons on the map of your life are not there to mark the boundaries of where you must stay—they are there to show you what you must slay! It's time to become a Dragon Slayer.

ACTIVATE THE WAY OF THE DRAGON SLAYER

DEFINE THE DRAGON

Like King Théoden in *The Lord of the Rings*, men have allowed themselves to be lulled into deception, passivity, and distraction. As a result, they are not playing their vital role as protectors, providers, and connectors in their families, communities, nation, and the world, and great evil and destruction is being perpetrated. We are living in an age of "weak men" who are creating "hard times":

> Hard times create strong men
> Strong men create good times
> Good times create weak men
> Weak men create hard times

Our call is to become "strong men" who face the discomfort of life and take on our manly responsibilities. Doing this requires us to face the fears that challenge us in each area of our primary relationships and responsibilities—God, ourselves, women, other men, nature, machines, and provision. These are the seven dragons that we must slay to rise as men of love, strength, and sacrifice who look like Jesus.

POINTS OF ATTACK

There are three primary manly roles we play in these seven areas:

- Provision: Using our creative skills and ingenuity to cultivate an area of fruitfulness that benefits others.
- Protection: Using our strength to confront threats to the vulnerable and weak.
- Connection: Using our leadership to create bonds of covenant, identity, and belonging in marriage, family, and community.

To be undermined in any of these three areas is a derailment in our masculinity. Our enemy works to get us to misuse or run away from these roles through temptation and intimidation.

LESSONS LEARNED

E.M. Bounds said, "Men are God's method. The church is looking for better methods; God is looking for better men." This is the description of "better men" I and my fellow Dragon Slayers have embraced and are pursuing in our lives:

> Men always protect
> They never exploit the weak
> Men always set the standard of love
> They never hate their enemy
> Men always provide resources, strength, and identity
> They never consume or compromise the quality of life for others
> Men always control themselves from the inside out
> They never control other people
> Men take full responsibility
> They never blame others or neglect their responsibilities

Men sacrifice for the benefit of others
They never sacrifice others for their own benefit
Men live submitted to other men
They never live as the masters of their own universe

THE SWORD

> Husbands, love your wives, just as Christ also loved the church and gave Himself for her . . . So husbands ought to love their own wives as their own bodies; he who loves his wife loves himself. (Ephesians 5: 25a, 28)

> "Listen to Me, you who follow after righteousness, You who seek the LORD:
> Look to the rock from which you were hewn, And to the hole of the pit from which you were dug." (Psalm 51:1)

> For you were once darkness, but now you are light in the Lord. Walk as children of light (for the fruit of the Spirit is in all goodness, righteousness, and truth), finding out what is acceptable to the Lord. And have no fellowship with the unfruitful works of darkness, but rather expose them. (Ephesians 5:8-11)

HOW TO SLAY

1. Reflect.

   a. Much of the way we fulfill or fail to fulfill our manly roles is due to what we saw modeled for us growing up. Who is your provider? Who protects you? Who is your primary source of unconditional love?

   b. Rank the order of success you hold in the roles of protector, provider, and connector—"1" being the role where you feel the strongest and "3" needing the most work.

   c. Consider the description of "better men" above. Are there any of these declarations that stir up a question or resistance for you?

2. Connect.

    a. Discuss your reflections on the questions above with the men you are with. Tell them what you will be doing differently.

3. Adjust.

    a. Your answer to these questions above will begin to reveal to you your God. If you discovered that "Me," "My wife," or anyone besides the Lord is your ultimate source of provision, protection, and connection, you've found a place to repent and put Jesus back into His rightful place of authority, influence, and leadership in your life.

    b. Consider the manly role you ranked as #3. What is one thing you could adjust today and make progress in this area?

CHAPTER 2

MAN WITH GOD

My friend Ron Adkins grew up in a home dominated by the fear of his father's physical and verbal violence. He never knew what infractions would trigger a beating—it could be something as minor as forgetting one of his father's tools in the yard. But the terrifying rage and abuse were so unbearable that by the age of fourteen, he decided to run away from home.

Ron soon took up with a band of young skinheads who roamed the neighborhoods of his Texas town breaking into houses, raiding drug dens, and generally getting into whatever trouble they could find. By the age of seventeen, he had built up a significant criminal record, and at nineteen, he stood trial for his many felonies. After reading his guilty verdict, the judge delivered Ron's punishment—five life sentences, each ninety-nine years, in prison.

Sitting in jail before transferring to the state prison, Ron had time to contemplate the shocking reality that he would be spending the remainder of his life "inside." Resentment, bitterness, self-hatred, and hopelessness consumed his heart as he accepted that he had brought this on himself. Terrorized by anger and violence as a boy, he had now become what he hated—angry and violent. Yet the only way to survive in prison, he reckoned, was to continue to be this person he had become even more fully.

And so, when he arrived at the penitentiary, he wasted no time in establishing himself as one of the most dangerous and deadly men there. He joined a prison gang and began racking up assault charge after assault charge against the guards and inmates. His infractions escalated over twelve years until they moved him to solitary confinement on a level three maximum security floor where they kept the criminally insane. For five more years, Ron waged an all-out war against the prison officers, who were the only people he had any contact with. They soon made it a policy to send a SORT—special operations response team—of six or more men in full riot gear to deal with him whenever they needed to take him from his cell to the shower or some other area. Before these encounters, Ron would invoke pagan "berserker" spirits that enabled him to break out of handcuffs, rip the guards' shields and clubs from their grasp, and cause as much damage as possible before they managed to subdue him with tear gas. Many times he came to after these fights with no memory of what had happened. Though deep down he hated himself for continuing to play a villain, he saw no way of escape from this identity and the destruction it demanded from him.

Eventually, Ron's prison crimes earned him a court date and the possibility of another life sentence. He was transferred to a super maximum security prison where his cell in solitary confinement had a shower and he no longer needed to be escorted anywhere. Completely alone, he began to imagine suicide like never before. By this point, he had read thousands of books in prison, exploring self-help, psychology, philosophy, and religion in a quest to try to manage his unrelenting rage and self-hatred, but nothing had brought the breakthrough he sought. In desperation, he finally cried out to the God he had told himself for years did not exist.

"God, if You're real, You're going to have to show me in no uncertain terms. Because I don't think I can believe in You. Show me who You are."

When Ron tells the story, he says that at this point, "Jesus walked into the cell with me." Though invisible, the presence and power of God were so tangible to him in that moment that he began to weep for the first time in nearly twenty years. As the tears flowed, Ron says, it was as though God reached into his heart, grasped the anger, bitterness, and resentment that had been firmly embedded there for so long, and pulled it up by the roots.

This encounter was nothing less than a miraculous deliverance. Like the Gadarene demoniac, Ron immediately changed from a raging monster to a man in his right mind, consumed with the desire to know everything he could about the One who had saved him from his internal torment. From that day on, he dedicated his time to prayer and Scripture. He renounced his leadership role in the prison gang and never committed another disciplinary infraction during his time in prison. He also successfully avoided the provocations of the guards who, refusing to believe his conversion was genuine, repeatedly tried to get him to revert back to violence to get him in trouble.

Three years after meeting the Lord, Ron learned that he had been scheduled for a parole interview. He was sure it had to be a mistake, as he was still eighty years away from even being eligible. But he went anyway, figuring it was at least a chance to go for a walk. A month later, an officer came to his cell with a piece of paper stating that he had been granted parole on all five of his ninety-nine-year sentences. However, he was still required to serve the five-year sentence he had earned for his prison crimes, and the officer assured him he would remain in solitary confinement for that time. Yet only eight months later, this too was reversed when Ron received permission to go through the Gang Renouncement and Dissociation (GRAD) program, which would rehabilitate and transition him back to the general prison population and officially make him an ex-gang member in the eyes of the Texas prison system.

After completing the GRAD program, Ron was transferred to a medium-security level prison called the Wynne Unit in Huntsville, Texas. A new prison ministry, the Joseph Company, was just graduating its first class of inmates from its school of supernatural ministry, and after learning what it was all about, Ron immediately signed up to be in the next class. It was in this school that Ron finally began to know God as a Father who was nothing like the father who had raised him. Instinctively, he had always imagined God to be just like his dad—ready to deal out anger, shame, judgment, and punishment at the slightest provocation. Even after encountering Jesus in his cell and being set free from torment, he still found it hard to believe that God wasn't just waiting to bring down the hammer on him if he messed up again. Yet the signs of God's grace—His unmerited favor—that had continually unfolded in his life from that encounter on were undeniable, and as he sat in class learning about the Father's heart for him, Ron finally began to see and believe that God was not an angry, judgmental punisher, but a loving, forgiving reconciler and restorer.

In 2015, after serving twenty-five years, Ron was released from prison. After being institutionalized for almost all of his adult life, he now faced a world that was vastly different from the one he had been banished from at nineteen. Smartphones, the internet, credit cards, and above all, freedom on a level he had never known all needed to be mastered as he learned to integrate into society and build a healthy and productive life. However, God had already set up a divine appointment to help Ron transition to his new reality.

On a Sunday morning, Ron walked into a small country church in Lone Oak, Texas, and was astonished to see the very same judge who had presided over his trial twenty-five years earlier—the judge who had handed down those five life sentences—present in the congregation. Even more shocking, the two of them started talking after the meeting. Ron was amazed to hear the judge's heart to see criminals encounter the transforming power of Jesus. At the end of the conversation, the judge invited Ron to come to his home group. Week after week in the judge's living room, they developed a relationship, and the man became a spiritual father in Ron's life.

The Father's favor has continued to chase Ron down, bringing him blessings beyond anything he had imagined for himself. His biggest dream was to have a family, which God fulfilled when he brought Dawn, a single mother of three, into his life. Dawn also has a powerful testimony of meeting the Lord in prison, and built a thriving women's ministry, Radical Restoration, which Ron continues to support. More recently, he's been invited back to the Wynne Unit to teach at the school of ministry, and to other prisons to speak at their GRAD programs. His growing passion is to see men and women in prison encounter the Father just like he did.

THE WAY OF THE DRAGON SLAYER

The Nature of the Dragon:
The Fear of Judgment, Punishment, and Unworthiness

Are you a criminal in a courtroom standing before a punishing judge, or a son in the living room standing before a loving father? This is perhaps the most critical theological question every man must answer, for it will define the story he believes he is living in and who he is in that story.

The problem is that we start to answer this question in childhood, and our answer is typically based not on our experience with God, but with our fathers. Some of us had good dads who connected with us and trained and disciplined us out of love, making it easier to see how God fathers us that way. But many of us had not-so-great dads. Some were like Ron's dad—angry, abusive, and intimidating—while others were distant, disengaged, or, like mine, totally out of the picture. Both experiences produce a distorted vision of God and ourselves. We end up seeing God, either as an angry, punishing, and somewhat arbitrary judge, or as coldly absent and disinterested in our lives. And we end up seeing ourselves as accused and condemned offenders, or as unloved, unworthy orphans who don't belong to anyone.

The main problem with both of these distorted views of God and ourselves is that they produce fear—not the "fear of the Lord" that leads us toward Him, but the fear of punishment, judgment, and unworthiness that leads us to keep Him at a controllable distance. This fear tells us that we aren't safe to approach God—either because we can't be sure that He's good, or that we are good enough to deserve His favor. This fear naturally causes us to live estranged from Him—or more accurately, to live at war with Him by refusing to give Him His rightful place as God in our lives.

The Dragon Behind Them All

This fear that drives us away from God originates in the ancient, cosmic war between God and His enemy, who Genesis 3 introduces as the *nâchâsh* or "serpent." The word also means the "hisser" or "whisperer," from a root word that means to practice divination, chant magic spells, and weave enchantments.[7] In the last book of the Bible, we get the "reveal" of who this character is: "The great dragon . . . that ancient serpent, who is called the devil and Satan, the deceiver of the whole world" (Revelation 12:9 ESV).

This "great dragon" is the dragon behind the seven dragons. He was already at war with God before we came on the scene, and from the moment God created mankind, we were caught up in that war, targeted by the enemy's primary weapon—his lying tongue. This is why each of our deepest fears about our relationships, roles, and responsibilities is rooted in a deception that comes from the father of lies.

Behind the first of the seven dragons—the one that stands between us and our Creator—is the most fundamental lie of all: *God cannot be trusted.* The enemy's sole agenda in entering the garden of God was to weave an enchantment that would get man to believe this lie. He knew that if he convinced man to mistrust God, he would break the one rule God had given him—not to eat of the tree of the knowledge of good and evil. That one rule existed not to prevent mankind from knowing about good and evil—God always intended to give humans all the knowledge and wisdom they needed to do good and defeat evil—but simply to establish that man had a Ruler. Man was created and designed in God's image to rule all of creation with God. But this delegated authority only worked because man remained faithfully operating under God's authority, doing things His way. As long as he refused to break that one rule, the man protected his relationship with the Ruler, and by extension, protected the relationships, roles, and realm he was created to rule. His power and authority, rightly used, caused everything he touched to become fruitful and flourish. The moment he decided to break that rule and try to be his own ruler, however, he didn't only violate his relationship with God—he shattered his relationships with himself, with the woman, with other men, with the created world, and with his work;

---

7 | "H5175 - nāḥāš - Strong's Hebrew Lexicon (esv)." Blue Letter Bible. Accessed 18 Sep, 2023. https://www.blueletterbible.org/lexicon/h5175/esv/wlc/0-1/; "H5172 - nāḥaš - Strong's Hebrew Lexicon (esv)." Blue Letter Bible. Accessed 18 Sep, 2023. https://www.blueletterbible.org/lexicon/h5172/esv/wlc/0-1/

perverted his role as provider, protector, and connector; and caused his power and authority to unleash pain, fruitlessness, frustration, and devastation.

When the man believed the dragon's lies about his relationship with God, his "eyes were opened" (Genesis 3:7). In fact, what he saw was a distortion—a filter of shame now colored his view of himself, while a filter of fear colored his view of God. He was "naked and afraid," no longer working to protect the garden as he was originally assigned, but scrambling to hide, cover, and protect himself from God. Tragically, he and all his descendents were now caught in the power of this deception. Since the fall, man has always gotten suckered into believing that he can do a better job of making the rules and being his own god, no matter how often it continues to backfire.

THE WAY OF THE DRAGON SLAYER

Riding the Dragon: Trying to Play God

When it comes to dealing with the dragon and his lies, we only have two options. We can either choose to *ride* the dragon, or *slay* the dragon. Riding the dragon is what happens when we allow the enemy's lies to build strongholds in our thinking and behavior. Slaying the dragon is what happens when we destroy those strongholds and build new ones on God's truth.

The comedy *Bruce Almighty* hilariously depicts what happens when we ride the first of the seven dragons and decide to play God in our own lives. Frustrated when things aren't going his way in life, Bruce blames God and accuses Him of being punishing and sadistic: "God is a mean kid sitting on an ant hill with a magnifying glass!" Convinced he could do a much better job running the world, he goes to war with God, finally calling Him out: "Smite me, O Mighty Smiter!" In a surprising turn of destiny, God shows up and gives Bruce a chance to run the world, with two conditions—he can't tell anyone he's God, and he can't mess with free will.

Upon discovering his new powers, Bruce immediately begins shaping his whole life to serve himself. Imagine the unchecked powers of the universe at your fingertips! Like a little boy who just discovered his . . . tongue, he stuffs as many pleasures as he can enjoy into his day. Eventually, he settles down to work answering prayer requests and soon decides to expedite them all with a "Yes." Certainly, everyone getting their way is the path to happiness. To his horror, social and economic chaos ensues. As the world comes crashing down around him, he realizes he can never represent a wise, benevolent, loving God with his finite capacity as a human being. Bruce finally reaches his breaking point and asks God to take His job back. He is then hit by a truck, and after "rising from the dead," finally sees that his life is about giving love, service, and joy to others.

If only we could be like Bruce and figure out our relationship with God in one movie. For most of us, it takes a lifetime to learn how to give God his rightful place and then be successful in staying off His throne. In the process, we will take this dragon for a ride, probably many times, before we learn to slay it. And unlike the movies, most of the time our dragon rides aren't very funny. Some of us become like the old Ron when we're riding this dragon—angry and ready to use aggressive force to get our way. Others become self-righteous, religious, controlling, and critical, while others stubbornly disengage from their own lives, relationships, roles, and responsibilities. Sadly, thanks to the nature of deception, many of us can't see the wake of destruction we are causing by choosing to use our power to serve ourselves.

Some of the most subtle dragon riders I have met are working in ministry. In my leadership role, I have often been called in to confront a leader when his marriage or ministry is falling apart. Typically, the initial story I hear is that someone else is the problem. The man is clearly a kind, humble, non-aggressive pastor, evangelist, or worship leader who serves God and people professionally, and his wife or team members just decided to get offended and leave for no reason. When I sit down with these leaders, their spouses, and colleagues, however, I soon uncover a very different story. This man's reputation, even if he sincerely believes it to be true, is a false cover. The people closest to him do not experience him as a kind servant, but as a selfish, controlling tyrant. Like the hiker Aron Ralston, who sawed his own arm off with a pocket knife after it became trapped under an 800-lb boulder (as depicted in the film *127 Hours*), these wives and colleagues, after so many years of enduring abuse or being deprived of their needs in the relationship, have finally become desperate enough to blow it up to survive. My job then becomes trying to show the man that he is the dragon rider responsible for this devastation, and that until and unless he decides to humble himself, repent, and step down from his false throne, I will have no option but to support these people in their journey of protecting themselves from him.

THE WAY OF THE DRAGON SLAYER

Facing the Dragon: Unraveling the Punishment Paradigm

The only way we go from riding to slaying the dragon is through *repentance*, which means to change the way we think and perceive reality. We can't just try to change our behavior—we have to drill down and confront the fears driving our behavior, and behind those fears, the lies we've believed for so long. With this first dragon, repentance means unraveling what I call the Punishment Paradigm and replacing it with a New Covenant paradigm (If you've read my book *Unpunishable*, this will be familiar).

The Punishment Paradigm is the reality we experience when our lives are operating in the ultimate punishment of them all—being disconnected from God. Being born into a fallen world, we are swiftly wounded by the realities of sin, pain, sickness, loss, and evil. These create the fertile ground in which the enemy can plant the seed of mistrust in God. These wounds also typically come through parents and authority figures who, through the behavior they punish and reward, teach us lies about how our relationships with people in authority are supposed to operate:

- Value and acceptance are earned and maintained through "good" behavior.
- Failure deserves to be punished with rejection, suffering, and disconnection.
- The experience of protective, nourishing love is only available when you are pleasing.

This relational template makes it easy for us to accept the dragon's deception that this is how it also works in our relationship with God:

- God is against us.
- We can't be sure that He is for our freedom, happiness, or destiny.
- The only relationship He will accept with us is one of subservience, slavery, and control.

These beliefs, and the fear of judgment, punishment, and unworthiness they produce, drive us toward behavior strategies with a singular goal: self-preservation. And where do the strategies of self-preservation lead us? Only to become the worst versions of ourselves—violent, controlling aggressors, narcissistic predators, or passive dropouts—and recreate the same dynamic of hurt that wounded us in the first place. Ron's adoption of the same tool his father used to punish him—violence—led him to unleash the same pain in the lives of dozens of other people. Likewise, whenever I have the privilege of walking with a leader who is taking a repentance journey, we inevitably find that his dragon-riding behavior is the result of his own efforts to survive the hostile environment in which he was originally wounded.

The Punishment Paradigm

IDENTITY	Criminal/Orphan
CORE BELIEF	God and other authority figures are unsafe and untrustworthy. My flaws and failures make me unworthy of love, belonging, and connection. I deserve disconnection and punishment. So does everyone else with flaws and failures.
MOTIVE	Fear of punishment (disconnection), judgment, unworthiness
BEHAVIOR STRATEGIES	Conform, lie, deny, blame, act like a victim, rebel, make the rules, self-justify, judge and punish ourselves and others
GOAL	Self-preservation

Jesus came to set us free from the Punishment Paradigm and lead us into the New Covenant Paradigm—not just by dying for our sin, but by *showing us the Father*. Everything He did and said drove home the truth that we can trust God, and showed what happens when we do. Unlike Adam, Jesus remained a faithful Son who refused to step out from under His Father's authority, even when the Father led Him through temptation, suffering, and death. The result? Jesus didn't just resist the dragon—He defeated him and exposed his lies for what they were. He showed us that the devil was, in fact, the true punisher, accuser, and tyrant who is always projecting his own nature onto God, while God is a loving Father who sacrificed everything to restore us back to relationship with Him.

Seeing the Father and the dragon for who they are will transform us, because it brings into focus who we are and how we can and ought to live. If God does not exist, then there is not much reason for me to exist either. If He is an aggressive enemy of my freedom, happiness, and peace, then I must reject Him with all my energy. If He couldn't care less about me, then I couldn't care less about Him. But, if those are all lies and He is in fact a loving Father who wants a deep, meaningful connection through which to unfold a powerful destiny, purpose, and authority in my life, well, that changes everything!

The New Covenant paradigm replaces the lies of the Punishment Paradigm with the truth:

- God is good, and He wants connection with us.
- Nothing can separate us from the love of God.
- Jesus has accepted all the punishment for our sins.
- The Father runs towards us in our repentance.

Moving from the Punishment Paradigm to the New Covenant Paradigm takes us from the courtroom to the living room. The fear of judgment, punishment, and unworthiness is "cast out" (John 4:18) by the new motive of love, which leads us to adopt a completely different set of behavioral strategies directed at the goal of connection, not self-preservation. We replace self-serving with self-sacrifice in service to God and others; rebellion with humility, trust, and submission to God's authority; blame-shifting and self-justification with repentance, reconciliation, and restoration; and aggressive dominance and passive cowardice with responsibility, engagement, and leadership.

THE NEW COVENANT PARADIGM	
IDENTITY	Son/Daughter of God
CORE BELIEF	My Father is good and I can trust Him completely. Through Jesus, I am worthy of love, belonging, and connection. My mistakes do not disqualify me from the Father's love. Instead, they are precisely where I learn the depth of His love, forgiveness, and commitment to transform me into a mature son/daughter who looks like Jesus.
MOTIVE	Love
BEHAVIOR STRATEGIES	Pursue and protect connection, even when it's scary, painful, or offensive. Clean up our messes that bring disconnection by following the path of repentance, reconciliation, and restoration opened to us by Jesus.
GOAL	Connection

The challenge is that while we have encounters with the Father like Ron had that life-changing day in solitary confinement, we do not move from the Punishment Paradigm to the New Covenant Paradigm in a moment. In our journey to walk in our true identity and relationship with our Father, we will face the dragon of judgment, punishment, and unworthiness more than once—until we learn to slay it completely.

THE WAY OF THE DRAGON SLAYER

The Way of the Dragon Slayer: Discipline and Dreams

My dad left before I could really remember him, leaving my mom to raise me. Over the years, a stream of her boyfriends passed through our house, but none were interested in being a father to me and most of them were scary, so I was happy to stay invisible to them. Many years later, as a social worker working with kids, I noticed that the kids who were neglected, abandoned, or orphaned often struggled more to engage with other people, especially adults, than kids who were actively abused by a caregiver, because the abused kids at least developed some social and relational tools (albeit dysfunctional ones) while the neglected kids had none. I wasn't quite an orphan because I had my mom around, but when it came to relating to other men, authority figures, or God, I was in a similar boat. I didn't have any tools, so I pretty much avoided them—until I became a Christian.

The first thing that surprised me about learning to relate to the Father was the *access* He offered me. I'll never forget the conversation I had with Kris Vallotton when I first gathered the courage to ask him, "So how do you go to church?"

"You just come," he said, looking a little puzzled by the question.

"You mean they're just going to let me walk into church?" I scoffed.

"Well, yeah," he said.

I couldn't believe that the "God club" just let in anyone off the street. But I went and met the Lord and when I started reading the Bible, I was shocked to read that He calls us to "come boldly to the throne of grace" (Hebrews 4:16). Not only was God there, not only did He give me free and complete access to His presence—He wanted me to come to him boldly, like I belonged there. It took me a while to wrap my brain around that, but eventually it dawned on me: this is how a son behaves when he understands he's in the living room with a loving father.

The other new thing I discovered in learning to relate to God was *accountability*. I still remember as a new Christian hearing Bill Johnson explain how he taught his children that they would one day give an account to God for what they did with their lives. This was a brand-new thought for me. Growing up, I had simply concluded that I didn't really have to answer to anyone for how I chose to live. This was, and continues to be, after all, the prevailing belief in secular American culture steeped in evolutionism (we are the product of dumb impersonal forces, not a Creator) and liberalism (freedom means doing whatever you want). Instead of being liberating, however, answering to nothing and no one higher than myself only left me lost, wandering in darkness without any great sense of purpose. It was only when I heard the story of the gospel, which told me that I had been created by God, ransomed from death by Jesus, and reconciled to the Father as His son, that I found the purpose and meaning my soul desired. This was the story that made sense and that I wanted to live in. But embracing it meant I was now responsible and accountable to this ultimate Authority in my life.

Accountability has become a dirty word in much of church culture because the church has been infected by criminal/courtroom/judge theology. When you're a criminal, accountability means you're on probation, trying to earn privileges and avoid punishment through good behavior. You have to surround yourself with a system to surveil and control you so you don't mess up again. But when you're a son, accountability is about stewardship, honor, and legacy. You're not trying to avoid mistakes, you're trying to bring honor to the family name by being a good representative of it. Your motive is not fear of getting caught, but love of what has been entrusted to you.

Journeying into a life of access and accountability to the Father will naturally lead us to confront this first dragon of fear in our lives. The fear of punishment, judgment, and unworthiness classically attacks when we feel disconnected or discouraged, when we've failed, or when we've betrayed our own hearts. When the voice of condemnation is loud, it's tempting to believe we are a criminal and not a son, and start to move away from rather than towards our Father. Our decision of what we believe in these moments will frame our spiritual life and determine victory or defeat in our battle with this dragon. The measure of our success is seen in how we are learning to love

God, ourselves, and others without fear: "There is no fear in love [dread does not exist]. But perfect (complete, full-grown) love drives out fear, because fear involves [the expectation of divine] punishment, so the one who is afraid [of God's judgment] is not perfected in love [has not grown into a sufficient understanding of God's love]" (1 John 4:18 AMP).

There are two areas of practice where we must confront and slay this dragon of fear as we grow in access and accountability. The first is learning to submit to *discipline* in our lives—usually through other men, spiritual fathers, or authority figures who offer us feedback, correction, and challenging assignments. The fear of judgment, punishment, and unworthiness always tries to frame discipline as a punishment designed to shame, control, or destroy us. If we listen to this fear every time it speaks, it will completely cut us off from our ability to learn, grow, and achieve self-mastery, because these only come within reach when we trust someone enough to open our lives to their influence.

Obviously, the main person we must learn to trust is the Father. We have to learn to let Him be God in our lives—to submit to Him as the Ruler, accept His standards and requirements for our lives, and follow Him where He leads us. But part of the Father's way of correcting the distorted lens through which we have seen Him is to bring healthy fathers and leaders into our lives who can walk with us and teach us what healthy authority looks like. Good fathering is caught more than taught, so if we want to become good fathers and leaders ourselves, we need to get around good fathers and leaders. Discipline and discipleship simply mean practicing being like our fathers who are imitating the Father, just as Paul instructed the Corinthian church: "Imitate me, just as I also [imitate] Christ" (1 Corinthians 11:1). Good fathers will give us access to their lives, but also require accountability from us—they want to see that we are taking the correction, wisdom, resources, opportunities, and encouragement they offer us and putting it to good use.

The second practical area in which we must slay this dragon of fear is learning to *dream* and pursue the desires of our hearts with God. Dreaming is another word, like accountability, that religious culture has perverted by clinging to criminal/courtroom/judge theology. Criminals don't really get to dream, or if they do, their dreams are extremely small and limited, because their hope and vision for the future is confined to a 10x10 cell. Religious culture has convinced so many people that that's the only space safe enough for them to live in—a space where we don't risk being disappointed by God or disqualifying ourselves through sin.

Imagine you had a big year at work and you want to spend your bonus on your kids for Christmas. You go to them and ask, "Hey, what do you want for Christmas? Sky's the limit."

Your child responds, "O Father, not my will but Your will be done. Will you pick out my Christmas presents?"

"No, honey, you don't understand. Ask me anything you want. What do you want?"

"O Father, lead me not into temptation, but deliver me from evil."

"Baby, what are you talking about? Have you been going to church? Where did you learn to see me like that?"

Jesus put it like this:

> "Ask, and it will be given to you; seek, and you will find; knock, and it will be opened to you. For everyone who asks receives, and he who seeks finds, and to him who knocks it will be opened. Or what man is there among you who, if his son asks for bread, will give him a stone? Or if he asks for a fish, will he give him a serpent? If you then, being evil, know how to give good gifts to your children, how much more will your Father who is in heaven give good things to those who ask Him!"
> (Matthew 7:7-11)

Sons in the living room don't just get to dream, they're trained and required to dream—not only about what they hope to experience and accomplish in their lifetime, but about the legacy they hope to leave for generations to come and into eternity. There's nothing our Father—like every good father—wants more than to see His kids pursue and fulfill the dreams of their heart, which are the expressions of their design and purpose. Psalm 126 says, "When the LORD restored the fortunes of Zion, we were like those who dream. Then our mouth was filled with laughter, and our tongue with shouts of joy; then they said among the nations, 'The LORD has done great things for them' (Psalm 126:1-2 ESV). In other words, genuine God dreams are designed to be a source of joy for us and a sign to the rest of the world that makes them go, "Who's your Daddy?"

The book of Proverbs equates dreaming with hope in a parallelism: "Hope deferred makes the heart sick, but a dream fulfilled is a tree of life" (13:12 NLT). My friend Steve Backlund often says (paraphrasing Francis Frangipane), "Any area of our lives that doesn't glisten with hope is under the influence of a lie." The converse is true—the more our lives glisten with hope, the greater we are walking in the truth of who God is and who we are. Dreaming is hope in action, which means when our dreams get small or stop, we're believing lies. We're living in captivity as criminals, not in freedom as sons. The dragon is taking us for a ride. Learning to dream with our Father through every season—loss and disappointment, fulfillment and abundance—is how we confront and slay the lies that God can't be trusted, or that we aren't worthy to be trusted.

Dreaming is a practice we must cultivate. Writing out our dreams is a good place to start. When I turned forty-one, it suddenly dawned on me that I was going to die one day. For whatever reason, I hadn't yet seriously contemplated this inevitability. Almost as soon as the awareness of my mortality descended on me, I heard the Lord say, "Write down a hundred dreams." Well, that didn't sound too difficult. I got out a piece of paper and pencil and started to write. After an hour and a half of writing, thinking, praying, thinking, praying, and thinking and praying some more, I counted up the list of dreams I had written down. *Ten.* Okay, this was going to be a little harder than I thought. But I persevered, and eventually I got a hundred dreams down on paper.

Habakkuk 2:2 says, "Write the vision; make it plain on tablets, so he may run who reads it" (ESV). The Message version says, "Write it out in big block letters so that it can be read on the run." God wanted my dreams to be something I was looking at as I was doing my life so I could pay attention to opportunities to move toward them, and best of all, to be delighted and amazed when He fulfilled them. In the last twenty years, I have seen God fulfill dozens of dreams from that original list, and many more I've added to it since. Sometimes I'll go through my list and realize there's a couple of dreams I had forgotten about that have come true. I may have forgotten, but God didn't. Some dreams seem inconsequential in the grand scheme of things—for example, one of the dreams I wrote down was that I wanted to go moose hunting. Not too long after I wrote it down, I got invited to Alaska to hunt moose. The first thing I ever shot was a moose, which now hangs on a wall in my house. God fulfilled that dream because He loves me and wants me to keep dreaming with Him. Every dream fulfilled is a kiss from a loving Father.

The journey of learning to dream with our Father is necessary for us to discover exactly what we have access to and what we are accountable for as His sons. The "good things" He wants us to ask Him for are usually beyond what we can ask or imagine, so He has to show them to us. I'll never forget my first trip to Brazil with Randy Clark, where I saw the blind see, the deaf hear, and the lame get up out of wheelchairs. After that trip I knew what I had access to as a son when I encountered people with these conditions. I could never again be content with merely hoping for them to experience anything less than the Father's miraculous power of restoration in their lives. Yet the Father has not asked me to start a miracle ministry like Randy's. I'm only accountable to steward the dreams He's given me. In this way, clarifying our dreams acts as a compass that helps us keep progressing towards our purpose. We don't get jealous of others because we know we have access to all things in our Father's house, but we also don't get distracted by others because we know what He's entrusted to us and what we're accountable for.

Discipline and dreaming are the hallmarks of a healthy relationship with our Father. Discipline expresses our desire to be with Him and be like Him, but discipline on its own will just make us robotic and compliant. Dreaming is how we express ourselves, but dreaming without discipline, and the partnership and purpose it brings, will only make us selfish and keep us from fulfilling our full potential. Together, discipline and dreaming mature us into being more like Him the more we become our true selves. In the process, we get to face off with punishment, judgment, and unworthiness until we no longer fear them, because we know our Daddy, and we trust Him.

ACTIVATE THE WAY OF THE DRAGON SLAYER

DEFINE THE DRAGON

Charles Spurgeon said, "Since the world was created, man has imitated Satan." The reason for this is that the fall of man removed his ability to see the Father as He truly is. We've taken on the perspective of a new father—Lucifer, the ruler of this world. It is the enemy who fears judgment, punishment, and unworthiness when he looks at God, and rightly so. His plan is to take as many of us down with him as he can, but God's plan through Christ is to redeem us from slavery, adopt us, and restore us to life in our true home, His kingdom. Our rebirth and resurrection in Christ gives us a new reality with a true experience with our heavenly Father. We are no longer unworthy orphans or condemned criminals but loved sons.

POINTS OF ATTACK

When these beliefs are embedded in our belief system, we will see God through the fear of judgment, punishment, and unworthiness:

- A holy God cannot stand to look at my flesh.

- He who sins must be punished.
- Sins separates us from being lovable or accepted.
- My dreams are probably not what God wants for my life.

Which of these lies seem to have the most impact on you when you are fighting through a failure or mistakes? Which of these feels like the most obvious area of attack in your life right now? How have you invited brothers in to fight with you?

LESSONS LEARNED

The New Covenant paradigm replaces the lies of the Punishment Paradigm with the truth:

- God is good, and He wants connection with us.
- Nothing can separate us from the love of God.
- Jesus has accepted all the punishment for our sins.
- The Father runs towards us in our repentance.

THE SWORD

Here are some powerful Scriptures to wield as you replace lies with truth:

> There is no fear in love [dread does not exist]. But perfect (complete, full-grown) love drives out fear, because fear involves [the expectation of divine] punishment, so the one who is afraid [of God's judgment] is not perfected in love [has not grown into a sufficient understanding of God's love]. We love, because He first loved us.
> (1 John 4:18-19 AMP)

For I am persuaded that neither death nor life, nor angels nor principalities nor powers, nor things present nor things to come, nor height nor depth, nor any other created thing, shall be able to separate us from the love of God which is in Christ Jesus our Lord. (Romans 8:38)

"A highway shall be there, and a road,

And it shall be called the Highway of Holiness.

The unclean shall not pass over it,

But it shall be for others.

Whoever walks the road, although a fool,

Shall not go astray." (Isaiah 35:8)

I have been crucified with Christ; it is no longer I who live, but Christ lives in me; and the life which I now live in the flesh I live by faith in the Son of God, who loved me and gave Himself for me. I do not set aside the grace of God; for if righteousness comes through the law, then Christ died in vain. (Galatians 2:20-21)

HOW TO SLAY

This is your reality in Christ: You wake up every day in the living room with your loving Father. You are never in the courtroom as a criminal before the judge. Deal with it!

1. Reflect.

    a. What is the strength of your connection with the Father today?

    b. Do you have any area to clean up a mess with the Father?

    c. What will you do today to strengthen your connection to the Father?

2. Connect. Tell this group of men what you will be doing to improve your connection to your Father.
3. Adjust. Do the 100 dreams exercise. Write them down, pray over them, post them somewhere visible, share them with friends.

CHAPTER 3
MAN WITH HIMSELF

Bob Hasson and I met over ten years ago, when his wife Lauren invited me to do a meeting for her regional ministry at their home in the San Diego area. At the time, I was limping around on a sprained ankle from falling down the stairs at St. Paul's Cathedral in London a couple of weeks earlier. While I sat in a chair with my foot propped up, Bob and I got to talking about guns, cars, and revivals. I learned that he loved shotguns and fast cars, and was intimately involved with the early years of the Vineyard Church movement, as well as a personal friend of Lonnie Frisbee. Bob asked if he could pray for my ankle. When nothing changed, he explained to me that he had given me one of his "time released" healing prayers. He was right! My ankle did feel much better a year later. We still laugh about that!

After hitting it off in that first conversation, Bob and I got to know each other well and soon became the best of friends. As we spent time together, I studied his style of relating to people and appreciated his obvious leadership gift. Bob was extremely hard-working and had built a large and successful commercial paint contracting business. He'd been surrounded by construction workers for decades and was a respected leader and expert negotiator in his industry. In the world of church and ministry, however, he was much more comfortable taking a supporting role to Lauren. He was not a fan of hanging around socializing with crowds of people at ministry events—more than once I heard him say, "I kind of hate people," and then laugh a little while scanning the room for an early exit. Yet whenever I had the opportunity to see Bob interacting with people, it was obvious to me that he carried a lot of wisdom and a huge father's heart.

Before long, I began inviting Bob to travel with me on ministry trips and encouraging him to consider working on a book project together. Several years before we met, I had released a book called *Culture of Honor* describing the power of honor in church culture. Many people asked if I would next write a book on how to bring honor into business culture, and I always said that would only happen if I met the right person in business to coauthor it with. Bob was reluctant at first, then agreed when he thought the book was primarily going to be my stuff with a few of his business stories sprinkled in. Once we started the book, however, it became clear that his voice, story, and expertise in business needed to be front and center. This created a bit of a dilemma for Bob. He had never imagined, much less sought, being in a position where he would be going so public with his personal journey. Yet uncomfortable as it was, he courageously rose to the challenge.

In our book, *The Business of Honor*, Bob tells the story of the most difficult season of his life, which took place in his mid-thirties. Over a couple of years, he and Lauren were devastated by a stillbirth and two miscarriages, and Bob's business nearly went bankrupt. These external losses were like a forest fire that ripped through Bob, and in the wake of destruction, caused seeds of guilt, shame, and inadequacy that had lain dormant inside him for many years to take root and grow. Bob simply knew, with unquestioning conviction, that these tragedies were somehow his fault. He had always known that he had a black heart, that he hadn't earned any of the good things in his life, and that all of this pain was him finally getting what he deserved. The only thing that remained to complete his punishment was for Lauren to leave him. In anticipation of this inevitable rejection, Bob began to drink regularly and heavily. He even shaved his head, as though he was already living in the prison his life would soon become. He became a man who was unrecognizable to everyone in his life, yet it was the man he had deep down always believed he was.

As day after day and week after week passed, however, the final blow Bob was bracing for never fell. Lauren did not leave him—instead, even as she wrestled with her own grief, depression, and bewilderment at her husband's behavior, she showed her love and loyalty to him in tangible, undeniable ways. Finally, a series of events, including a near-death experience, caused lightbulbs to start to pop on for Bob. What was he doing? Who had he become? He went to work to find answers to these questions, attending twelve-step meetings and counseling, while also trying to clean up his mess with his wife and family.

Through much prayer, counsel, and self-examination, Bob began to excavate and confront a series of lies he had believed about himself since boyhood—lies drilled into him by his father, who regularly reminded Bob, with many vicious and shaming epithets, that he couldn't do anything right. Even after coming to the Lord and doing his best to live a life of integrity, honor, generosity, and goodness, at his core Bob was still running from his father's wounding words. He had no trouble believing that other people deserved good things and were blessed by God—he just couldn't believe he did. He was fatally inadequate, and therefore disqualified from a life of success, fruitfulness, blessing, and legacy. As Bob began to uproot these lies and replace them with the healing words of his heavenly Father, he finally began to build a whole new set of beliefs that aligned with who he really was.

What's interesting is that when I met Bob, that tough season had been in his rearview for many years. He'd rebuilt his business and his marriage, and both were successful, blessed, and thriving. Yet when I invited him to put his story in a book, because there would be many who could relate to, learn from, and be encouraged by it, Bob experienced another challenge to his beliefs about himself. It was one thing to know that God had led him through a healing process that had saved his life. It was another thing to step into a position of authority and invite others to follow him in taking that journey. Though it was nothing as fierce as the knock-down, dragout fight he had endured decades earlier, Bob found himself needing to go a couple more rounds in the ring with the lies he used to believe as he wrote, published, and promoted our book. Yet again, God showed up to confirm the truth of who Bob was, deepening his conviction in his identity and giving him the courage to share the spoils of his victory with the world.

The Bob I know today is different from the man I met over a decade ago. He's still running his company, supporting Lauren in her endeavors, and loving his kids and now a couple of grandkids. But he's also stepped into a new position of authority and visibility in ministry. He's written a couple more books, started a successful podcast with Shawn Bolz, launched a church with Lauren and Jesus Culture in San Diego, and speaks and consults regularly with individuals and teams in the church and corporate worlds. The wisdom and father's heart I saw in him from the moment we met are now seen by everyone around him. Just as importantly, when Bob looks at himself, he sees them too.

THE WAY OF THE DRAGON SLAYER

The Nature of the Dragon: The Fear of Inadequacy, Self-Hatred, and Disqualification

This dragon we face when we look in the mirror is probably the one that shows up most often, and for the longest period of time. It haunts even the most successful, celebrated, and wisest men among us. This is why one of the most common issues leaders and CEOs struggle with is imposter syndrome, the tormenting fear that they don't actually have what it takes to fulfill their leadership role, and sooner or later everyone is going to find out. So many men go their whole careers climbing the ladder of professional success, hoping that when they get to the top, they'll finally feel like they belong, only to find the same old insecurities dogging their steps. I once saw the late Dr. Jack Hayford stand before 1,500 pastors at his annual pastoral leadership gathering in Van Nuys, CA and share that even though he was now in his seventies, he still occasionally experienced what he called "inadequacy seizures," times when he felt like he was drowning in his own sense of personal failure. This was a man who led one of the most prominent and successful Christian denominations in the world, The International Church of the Foursquare Gospel established by Aimee Semple Mcpherson in the early 1900s, directed the New King James Bible translation project, founded King's College and Seminary, and took a church of eighteen and turned it into more that 10,000 in attendance. A man as accomplished and respected as Dr. Hayford was still beating back the voices of inadequacy and disqualification.

When a man goes after himself, it's unfair in every sense of the word. He knows all the failings, weaknesses, fears, flaws, and dumb ideas this guy has ever had. These are *facts* we are dealing with, not just accusations. There seems to be nowhere to hide when the accuser comes to punish the man. He is laid open and vulnerable to the memories and circumstances connected to this barrage of "truth."

How many of these accusations have you been assaulted by?

"You screwed that up completely."
"You are failing to get so many important
    things done."
"You are way behind where you should be by now."
"You cannot work hard enough or long enough."
"You will always be in debt."
"You are a disappointment."
"You are unworthy of love."
"You are fundamentally flawed in your character
    and untrustworthy."
"You will never change."
"No one really enjoys you."
"You've looked at other women."
"Your children are afraid of you."
"Your son thinks you are a fool."
"Your daughter wants to get away from you."
"You are unavailable."
"You are not present."
"You hide from your wife and kids."
"You are moments away from being totally broke."
"You do not know what you are doing."

This list could go on and on. The fear that lives between the man we want to be and the man we believe we are is the fear of inadequacy, self-hatred, and disqualification. In our core, we all desire to be good, competent, effective, powerful, and successful as men. As John Eldredge puts it in *Wild at Heart*, every man wants to be convinced, "I have what it takes." We especially want others to see us that way, because we hope convincing other people will convince us we're really who we want to be. But thanks to our intimate knowledge of all our flaws and failures, it's easy for our fear to overwhelm our desire. And instead of facing it, many of us spend far too many years riding this dragon.

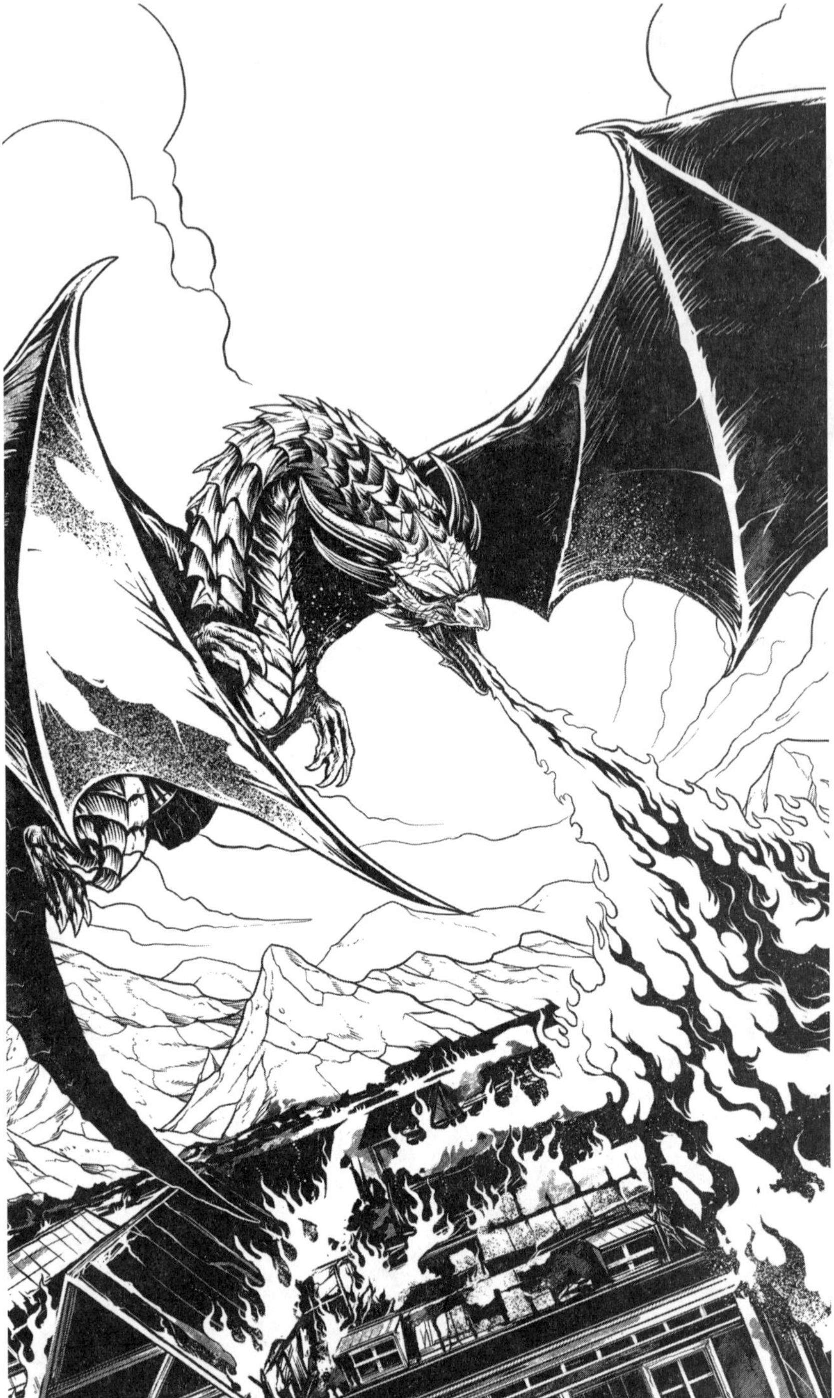

Riding the Dragon: Projection, Isolation, and Self-Medication

One of the ironies about dealing with the dragon of inadequacy, self-hatred, and disqualification is that most of us try to fight it in the dark. We think we know ourselves better than anybody, and develop behavior strategies to get what we want and need, while in fact possessing no actual self-awareness that our entire personality and the way we "happen" in our lives is built on insecurities. As long as we are operating out of this false identity, we are bound to be fighting the wrong battle—against God, others, the world, and even the devil—unaware that the true fight is between our true self and the fear-driven fantasy self we're doing everything to prop up.

As we've seen, men classically react to fear with fight or flight, aggression or passivity. The aggressive version of riding this dragon looks like a man working hard to project an image of power and success that will attract or intimidate people into rewarding him for being powerful and successful. Many of these aggressive dragon riders are heavily invested in chasing a vision of themselves that involves a popular bourbon; biceps, pecs, and quads; a jacked-up truck, sub-three-second 0-to-60 sports car, and other expensive toys; an entourage of beautiful women; and a corner office, give or take a few details. It's often a version of him succeeding in the traditional manly roles of provider, protector, and connector, but distorted by making these roles all about himself.

While the aggressive dragon rider hides behind the image he is projecting, the passive dragon rider just hides. An expert at keeping a low profile and dodging or deflecting attention, he doesn't even give other people the chance to notice or point out that he's simply opting out of manly roles. While both aggressive and passive dragon riders isolate themselves and develop weapons and armor to avoid all exposure of their insecurities, the passive rider is a master of isolation.

A man alone is a vulnerable man, due to his own self-deception. Proverbs 18:1 in the Amplified Bible says, "He who [willfully] separates himself [from God and man] seeks his own desire, He quarrels against all sound wisdom." He thinks he is the master of his universe, and therefore cannot accept it when the real universe tries to intrude. He becomes a closed system like a rancid pond. Nothing comes in and nothing goes out that he doesn't control. When anyone tries to confront his delusion, he self-justifies, denies, and defends his version of reality.

Along with being deceived, both the aggressive man and passive man are also in pain, and blind to the reality that their hiding and isolation are actually making the pain worse. Rather than expressing the pain honestly to people who could listen, empathize, and support, they seek to self-medicate with porn, alcohol, work, sex, adrenaline, food, or some other distraction they think they can control. Insecurity, projection, and isolation have now set the stage for an addiction. Unwittingly, they have fashioned themselves a cage and then furnished it with what they believe they need to survive it.

In his 2015 viral *HuffPost* article, "The Likely Cause of Addiction Has Been Discovered, and It Is Not What You Think," Johann Hari argues that addiction is more about self-medicating ourselves to survive a painful environment more than chasing a high.[8] He cites Bruce Alexander's "Rat Park" experiments from the 1970s, which proved that when rats were moved from a cage with only cocaine to a cage where they could socialize with other rats, they hardly ever took cocaine. That same decade they saw the same thing play out with soldiers coming home from Vietnam—ninety-five percent of those who used heroin regularly while enduring the war gave up the habit when they returned home to the States. Hari concludes that the biggest problem driving drug addiction in the West today is the epidemic of loneliness and isolation that has overtaken our culture. The most painful environment, it turns out, is being alone with ourselves. What he doesn't address in the article, however, is the problem that loneliness and isolation are largely self-inflicted by dragon riding men who can't see that their reaction to pain is just as destructive as the wound that originally caused it.

[8] | Johann Hari, "The Likely Cause of Addiction Has Been Discovered, and It Is Not What You Think," *HuffPost*, January 20, 2015, updated April 18, 2017, https://www.huffpost.com/entry/the-real-cause-of-addicti_b_6506936.

Relationships for men whose lives are built around medicating and avoiding their fear of inadequacy, self-hatred, and disqualification are recipes for hurt and heartbreak. They're like a dare—"Sure, go on and try to love the guy I've secretly hated most of my life and done everything to hide from the world. We'll be great as long as you feed my ego and never expose my vulnerability. The moment you cross that line, be ready for punishment and disconnection. Good luck!"

It's difficult to decide which of these dragon riders is more dangerous or destructive. Because they risk being visible, and indeed demand the spotlight, the aggressive dragon riders end up getting a lot more press for their ego-driven exploits. But the passive dragon riders, as we've seen, cause just as much damage. Jordan Peterson said it like this: "If you think strong men are dangerous, you should see what weak men are capable of." Again, strong (aggressive) men typically like to project a warped image of the manly provider, protector, and connector, but weak (passive) men abdicate these roles and will shapeshift into whatever the crowd or authorities are telling them to be in the name of self-preservation and maintaining some semblance of control. When forced to choose, weak, passive men will not fight evil—they will join it to preserve themselves.

If you want to know what weak men are capable of, you might want to read *Ordinary Men: Reserve Police Battalion 101 and the Final Solution in Poland* by Christopher Browning. This true story is a sad and stunning picture of what weak self-deception in the name of self-preservation will do to a man. At the beginning of World War II, middle-aged men who were less than fit for military enlistment were recruited as policemen to serve during the Nazi invasion of Poland. These reservists were akin to our National Guard in our local states and communities in the USA. In typical fashion, the higher-ups began sending orders down the military chain of command until these reserve units were activated. Dentists, salesmen, mechanics, bankers, and shopkeepers were given instructions to begin hunting and executing the Jews of their communities. These unlikely mass murderers were directly responsible for the deaths of 38,000 men, women, and children by mass shootings, and another 45,200 through collecting people from the ghettos and forcing them onto trains headed for concentration camps. Only about 10% of the total men refused or declined the orders given them. Meanwhile, the other 90% both engaged in the brutal murders and ridiculed, taunted, and punished those of their own who refused to comply.

Everywhere we look, we can find evil men on both sides of the aggressive-passive relationship. Cartels send drugs and prostitutes to the market, and drug addicts and porn users consume them. Power-hungry tech titans pour massive resources and energy into designing tools that lazy men can use to successfully retreat into a virtual reality and delegate their thinking and decision-making to algorithms and artificial intelligence. The common agreement on both ends of this supply and demand is that resources and people are to be sacrificed and used for the man, rather than the man sacrificing himself and becoming a resource for others. This self-focus is the theme in all the dragons we ride, but with this particular dragon it's all about creating a reality where a man never has to face his deepest fears about himself.

THE WAY OF THE DRAGON SLAYER

Facing the Dragon: Remember Who You Are

The ultimate goal of overcoming the fear of inadequacy, self-hatred, and disqualification is to develop a secure, authentic identity that can grow and expand over the course of your life. The journey of manhood encompasses many stages, each of which adds new experiences and roles to who we are. Various writers have described these stages in different ways. For example, in his book *Fathered by God,* John Eldredge suggests that there are six primary stages in a man's life: Boyhood, Cowboy, Warrior, Lover, King, and Sage. The idea is that at each stage, we are initiated into a new facet of our identity as a man, and each initiation requires a confrontation with our wounds and insecurities, another faceoff with this dragon of ourselves. The key to victory in each confrontation is the same: *we must remember who we are.*

This is the theme of the classic movie *Hook.* The film imagines a Peter Pan who has broken his vow to never grow up and left Neverland for the real world. Somewhere in the process of becoming a man, husband, and father, however, Peter has forgotten who he is so completely that he now has a phobia of flying. Worst of all, he has become a version of his old nemesis, Captain Hook, neglecting his family to pursue conquests in his job as a mergers and acquisitions lawyer. When his family reunites with Wendy, who is now grandmother to Peter's children, and Peter's son Jack describes to her what his father does at work, she looks at Peter in disappointment and says, "Peter, you've become a pirate."

Somehow knowing that Peter has returned to Wendy's house, Captain Hook forces him to renew their ancient battle by abducting his children from the very bedroom where he decided to abandon Neverland. Tinker Bell shows up to fly him back to the world of his forgotten childhood, dropping him off on the pirate ship where Hook has his kids strung up in a net. Caught flat-footed, Peter earns mockery and then disgust from Hook when he reveals that he is no longer Hook's "great and worthy opponent" who used to be able to "fly, fight, and crow." None of the tools he's cultivated to be powerful as a lawyer can help him in this battle. His only hope is to remember that he is The Pan, and by remembering, to recover his old abilities.

Hook gives Tinker Bell three days to help Peter accomplish this feat. While she's having the Lost Boys whip Peter into shape, Hook goes to work trying to poison Peter's children against him. Finally, Peter stumbles upon his old treehouse and the memories of his adventures with Wendy come flooding back, along with the reason why he decided to leave Neverland and grow up—he wanted to be a father. As the images of him holding a newborn Jack fill his mind, he suddenly realizes that he's flying! He's found his "happy thought," and with it, his true identity and power. He leads the Lost Boys into battle, defeats Hook, and wins back the hearts of his kids—no longer as the boy Peter Pan who fought, flew, and crowed for the fun of it, but now as the man Peter who now does it to protect what he loves.

In many ways, Hook's act of provoking Peter into battle is the best thing that could have happened to him. In our lives, it's a blessing when circumstances reveal the weakness of the false identity we've been living with and force us to go looking for our true selves. Peter's three days are symbolic of death and resurrection. We must surrender the false to receive the real, and this is not a comfortable process, because it requires us to face the thing that made us forget in the first place. *Hook* leaves this part out of Peter's story, but in our experience, self-amnesia doesn't happen without a reason—usually some form of wounding or trauma, especially childhood trauma. The process of giving up the denial and other coping strategies we've developed to help us avoid these painful experiences and finally confronting them is perhaps the greatest emotional and spiritual challenge in our lives.

In *Living from the Heart Jesus Gave You*, Jim Wilder breaks down the two types of wounds or traumas we can experience growing up. Type A traumas are experiences we needed but were absent from our lives, while Type B traumas were hurts or abuse actively perpetrated on us.

Examples of Type A traumas:

1. Not being cherished and celebrated by one's parents simply by virtue of one's existence.
2. Not having the experience of being a delight.
3. Not having a parent take the time to understand who you are – encouraging you to share who you are, what you think and what you feel.
4. Not receiving large amounts of non-sexual physical nurturing – laps to sit on, arms to hold you, and a willingness to let you go when you have had enough.
5. Not receiving age-appropriate limits and having those limits enforced in ways that do not call your value into question.
6. Not being given adequate food, clothing, shelter, medical and dental care.
7. Not being taught how to do hard things – to problem solve, and to develop persistence.
8. Not given opportunities to develop personal resources and talents.[9]

Examples of Type B traumas:

1. Physical abuse, including face slapping, hair pulling, shaking, punching, and tickling a child into hysteria.
2. Any spanking that becomes violent, leaving marks or bruises or emotional scars.
3. Sexual abuse, including inappropriate touching, sexual kissing or hugging, intercourse, oral or anal sex, voyeurism, exhibitionism, or the sharing of the parent's sexual experiences with a child.
4. Verbal abuse or name-calling.
5. Abandonment by a parent.

9 | Wilder, E. James; Friesen, James G.; Bierling, Anne; Koepcke, Rick; Poole, Maribeth. *Living From The Heart Jesus Gave You: 15th Anniversary Study Edition* (p. 85). Shepherd's House, Inc.. Kindle Edition.

6. Torture or satanic ritual abuse.
7. Witnessing someone else being abused.[10]

Sadly, most of us can point to one or more items on this list in our own histories. These experiences and their effects on us are what we must face to discover, heal, and integrate our true selves. The real damage of trauma is the narrative it creates in our minds. In every case of unresolved trauma, we are carrying around a story about ourselves that paints us as unsafe, vulnerable, guilty, shameful, bad, weak, powerless, unworthy, unloved, or rejected. In Bob's case, for example, the story was, "You can't do anything right. Everything bad is your fault." It is actually this lie about ourselves that creates the most acute pain and triggers our brains and souls to marshal whatever coping mechanism we can grab onto in order to survive. Ironically, however, so often these coping mechanisms are self-sabotaging and only lead to that core wound being re-inflicted and the lie being confirmed over and over again.

In his bestselling book on trauma, *The Body Keeps the Score*, psychiatrist Bessel van der Kolk describes a type of therapy called *internal family systems therapy* or IFS that sheds some light on how trauma affects our personalities and produces self-hatred and self-destructive behaviors. It's based on the idea that our self is actually made up of many facets or parts that operate like a family or relational network. Trauma, especially in childhood, causes these parts to become dissociated, fractured, and in conflict with each other:

> Trauma injects [the] parts [of our self-system] with beliefs and emotions that hijack them out of their naturally valuable state. For example, we all have parts that are childlike and fun. When we are abused, these are the parts that are hurt the most, and they become frozen, carrying the pain, terror,

---

10 | Wilder, E. James; Friesen, James G.; Bierling, Anne; Koepcke, Rick; Poole, Maribeth. *Living From The Heart Jesus Gave You: 15th Anniversary Study Edition* (p. 88). Shepherd's House, Inc.. Kindle Edition.

> and betrayal of abuse. This burden makes them toxic—parts of ourselves that we need to deny at all costs. Because they are locked away inside, IFS calls them *exiles*.
>
> At this point other parts organize to protect the internal family from the exiles. These protectors keep the toxic parts away, but in doing so they take on some of the energy of the abuser. Critical and perfectionistic *managers* can make sure we never get close to anyone or drive us to be relentlessly productive. Another group of protectors, which IFS calls *firefighters*, are emergency responders, acting impulsively whenever an experience triggers an exiled emotion . . . The critical insight is that all of these parts have a function: to protect the self from feeling the full terror of annihilation.[11]

According to this approach, self-hatred and self-rejection are actually part of a misguided and ultimately destructive survival strategy. We don't actually hate the true self that is the core and essence of our being. But we hate the vulnerable boy who was too weak to defend himself against abuse or to figure things out on his own when the experiences he needed were missing. We make inner vows that we will never be that weak, powerless, or exposed again. Up go the internal battlements in our soul, guarded by the prison wardens whose entire job is to keep that boy under lock and key. The key phrase is that our "protectors . . . take on some of the energy of the abuser." Through our isolation, addictions, self-aggrandizement, self-indulgence, and other self-protective behavior in relationships, we are actually punishing that

---

11 | Bessel van der Kolk, *The Body Keeps the Score* (New York: Penguin Books, 2014) 283-284.

boy inside us who taught us that we weren't safe, worthy, valuable, loved, protected, delighted in, and believed in. The goal in IFS therapy is to help us access our true self, disentangle it from the "exiled" boy and misguided internal protectors that have been waging a nonstop gang war inside us, and help them to make peace by giving each of them a message of acceptance, love, and understanding.

The film *The Adam Project* contains a beautiful and creative depiction of this journey of self-reconciliation. The story begins with an adult Adam Reed going back in time to stop his physicist father, Louis, from inventing time travel. Miscalculating, he arrives the year after his father's death and meets his twelve-year-old self, for whom he clearly has little compassion or liking. As the two of them team up to go back a few more years in time and find their dad, the adult Adam reveals that his tough guy persona is largely the product of his resentment toward his younger self for being too weak to defend himself from bullies or cope after his father's death, and toward his dad for not being there for him during that vulnerable time of life. In a series of scenes, the boy Adam confronts his older self for becoming angry instead of allowing himself to feel sadness; the older Adam feels compassion and fondness for his younger self; and his father, who after they track him down quickly deduces that he will not be there to see his son become a man, looks his grown son in the face and says all the things that he wants him to hear: "You're my son, Adam, and I love you. You're my boy, and I love you. I loved you from the first minute that I saw you, and that will never change. Adam, you're my boy. You're amazing. I love you. I am proud of you. I love you, son. Know that inside your heart... Don't carry this around anymore."[12] The father, young son, and adult son embrace, weeping as their love and grief can finally be expressed, their wounds healed, and their relationships reconciled.

This story points to the truth that when it comes to facing the wounded boy inside you, feeling compassion and love for him, and finding the tools to reparent him so he finally gets what he has needed for so long, you usually

---

12 | *The Adam Project*, directed by Shawn Levy (Netflix, 2022).

need a father figure to help you fill the gap. As believers, we have direct access to the Father, who will fill that gap perfectly. However, most of us also need help learning to go to Him to receive the words of love and truth that will heal our hearts. This is where inner healing ministry tools are so helpful. The "Father Ladder" is one inner healing tool that helps us to remove the lies we have believed about God so we can reconnect with Father, Son, and Holy Spirit. As we'll see throughout this book, the journey of facing these dragons is cumulative, because they're all connected. Slaying the dragon of fear between ourselves and God is critical in our journey to slay this dragon between us and the self, because reconnecting with Father, Son, and Holy Spirit plugs us directly into the source of the love and truth we need to love ourselves. Most importantly, it is in relationship with our Father that we can receive the only secure foundation for our identity. He is the only authority higher than ourselves who can tell us who we are, and He says of us as He says of Jesus: "This is my beloved son, with whom I am well pleased" (Matthew 3:17 ESV). Learning how the Father sees and feels about us necessarily forces us to acknowledge that what we've believed about that wounded boy inside us is a complete fabrication we were sold by the enemy of our souls. We also see what that boy needed and still needs from God and from us—acceptance, compassion, forgiveness, protection, guidance, and love.

THE WAY OF THE DRAGON SLAYER

The Way of the Dragon Slayer: Knowing Yourself

My friend Allen Cardines, Jr. is a man who manifests a wonderful degree of self-knowledge and self-acceptance, as evidenced by the fact that the people around him feel accepted for who they are. Acceptance is a gift we must receive for ourselves before we can really give it away. Allen pastors a church in Hawaii. Some years back, Allen told me a story about a funeral service he had officiated for a member of his congregation, which beautifully captured his security in who he is and his freedom to be himself.

In 2014, a well-dressed lady walked into Allen's church and introduced herself in a rather deep voice as "Chynna." Allen soon learned that Chynna was in fact a transsexual man who was hungry to know more about Jesus and also happened to be battling stage four cancer. He began to pray for Chynna's salvation, and it wasn't long before Chynna prayed to accept Jesus as Lord and Savior.

In early 2016, Chynna's cousin reached out to Allen to let him know that Chynna was dying in the hospital. Allen called and reminded Chynna of the truth of the gospel just before Chynna went home to be with Jesus. The next Sunday, a couple of Chynna's friends visited Allen's church and thanked him for sharing the love of God with Chynna, explaining that Chynna had been sharing that love in the LGBT community. A week or so later, some members of Chynna's family called Allen and explained that Chynna had specifically requested that he officiate the celebration of life service. They also told him that he would be the only "straight" person speaking at the celebration. He readily accepted the opportunity and began to pray for God to give him the right words to share with those attending.

Allen opened his talk at Chynna's funeral by calling out the elephant in the room. "I heard I was going to be the only straight person speaking tonight. I've been happily married to my beautiful wife, Mari, for twenty-one years," he said, gesturing to his wife on the front row, who was already looking uncomfortable. "But I need to get one thing off my chest. I am not straight!"

At this, every eye in the room became fixed on Allen, and his wife looked like she wanted to hide under the pew. "I am not straight!" he repeated. "I am crooked. The only straight person who walked the planet was Jesus Christ. Every single one of us is crooked. We are all sinners, separated from God, and in need of repentance. And we are all loved by God and of inestimable worth, which is why Jesus died to save us and give us a new life in Him. Chynna understood this and made Jesus Christ Lord and Savior. You can do the same right here tonight."

When Allen gave an altar call at the end of his talk, multiple people came forward to give their lives to Christ. A few weeks later, Allen received a call from Chynna's dad, Ronald, who said in a voice full of emotion, "My son was always looking for a man to love. Because of you, he found the love of Jesus and now I know I will see my son again in heaven."

I think you have to be pretty secure in your identity as a man and in the love of God to stand up in a room of men dressed up as women and say, "I'm not straight," without any pandering or people-pleasing, and with genuine love and compassion. Allen is a genuine, joyful man who truly loves people and doesn't need to put on a false front to win acceptance or cover his imperfections. He's free to let people see him because he knows he's fully loved and accepted by God, and therefore can love and accept himself.

Men like Allen prove that it is possible to move from being driven by the fear of self-annihilation, and the life of endless consumption it produces, to the love-driven rhythms of emptying ourselves, being filled, and emptying ourselves again. This is the ultimate evidence that we are slaying this dragon in our lives, and it also happens to be the lifestyle Jesus modeled for us. Completely secure in who He was and confident in His mission from the Father, He emptied Himself for us in life and death, as Paul urged us to imitate in these famous verses:

> Think of yourselves the way Christ Jesus thought
> of himself. He had equal status with God but

> didn't think so much of himself that he had to cling to the advantages of that status no matter what. Not at all. When the time came, he set aside the privileges of deity and took on the status of a slave, became *human*! Having become human, he stayed human. It was an incredibly humbling process. He didn't claim special privileges. Instead, he lived a selfless, obedient life and then died a selfless, obedient death—and the worst kind of death at that—a crucifixion. (Philippians 2:6-8 MSG)

Contrary to popular association, "humility" and "selflessness" are not qualities we develop by thinking less of ourselves or putting ourselves down. Humility is the fruit of self-awareness—the kind of self-awareness that only comes from comprehending the paradoxical truth about ourselves. As men, we are infinitely small in comparison to God, and yet He has elevated us as sons, princes, and rulers of His creation. As fallen men we are weak, deceived, and capable of sin, betrayal, and evil, yet as men created in the image of God and redeemed at the cost of His Son's life, we are infinitely loved and called to play an irreplaceable role in the redemptive history of mankind. Nothing both humbles and elevates us more than encountering the reality that we are prized by the greatest Person in the universe. It is this revelation that enables us to become "selfless," in the sense of being able to love and esteem others above ourselves (again, without needing to denigrate our own worth) and dedicate our focus, energies, and resources to their benefit.

Becoming humble and selfless is not easy. It requires us to do "the work"—acknowledging and owning our destructive behavior, confronting our painful emotions and the traumas behind them, and walking through a healing, forgiveness, repentance, and reconciliation process with God, ourselves, and others that ultimately replaces inadequacy, self-hatred, and disqualification with the convictions: "I am enough. I am loved. And I am qualified for everything I was created to be and do." We also have to come to the end of our flawed efforts to change ourselves and clean up our messes through externals—apologizing, behavior modification, and paying penance. We must acknowledge that our problem is with the man in the mirror, and until we reconcile with him, we will continue to take our internal war wherever we go.

There are three essential practices that every man should incorporate as they do "the work." First, find someone to work with—a coach, counselor, or mentor—and men to walk with. This healing journey must be self-led, but we can't do it alone—we need God's help and the help of others to heal from, make peace with, and embrace our story and identity. Often the kindest thing we can do for ourselves and our important relationships is to look for someone to talk to who isn't deeply involved in our lives already and can help us find the fresh perspective and truth we're looking for. I recommend seeing a good Christian therapist, scheduling some sessions for inner healing prayer ministry, joining a men's community, or attending a healing conference, retreat, or intensive.[13] We also need to surround ourselves with men we will walk in the light with, men who see us and can call us higher (more on this in Chapter 5).

Second, learn to practice solitude. Solitude is an ancient spiritual practice in which you commune with your own soul and spirit and the Holy Spirit through self-reflection and prayer. It sounds simple, but in the day of smartphones and endless distractions, it takes real self-discipline to carve out time to internally process and pray! Jesus Himself frequently retreated from His disciples and the crowds to be alone and pray, returning each time with fresh energy and clarity about His next ministry assignment. While it's valuable and important to have people to process with and bounce stuff off of, it's also important for us to process with ourselves and God. Solitude is where we can unpack any fear, anxiety, anger, overwhelm, or hopelessness

---

[13] | I especially recommend BraveCo with Jason Vallotton, Riding High Events with Todd Pierce, and books by Stephen Mansfield, John Eldredge, and Brant Hansen.

we've been carrying and get refilled with peace, joy, love, and hope. It's also where we can recalibrate and realign with the truth of our identity, vision, and mission. A few years ago, I recorded a series of guided meditations for a meditation app, Soultime, that specifically included an exercise for this purpose. At the end of the meditation, you would simply ask yourself and the Lord three questions: "What lie am I believing? Do I need to forgive anyone? What is the truth I need to believe?" On that note, if you want tools for building your solitude practice, there are tons of great devotionals, prayer journals, guided meditations, personality assessments, and other resources out there—keep looking till you find the right ones for you.

Third, declare the truth over yourself. Create a list of declarations from the "aha" moments in your self-discovery and healing journey. Write them down, post them on your mirror or places you see regularly, speak them aloud, and meditate on them. Here are some I have found effective for me and others:

> My God is powerful!
> My God is with me!
> My God has called me!
> My God works all things together for my good!
> I slay every day!

None of us can form new beliefs, brain pathways, or behavior that align with our true identity without this repetition. Declaring the truth consistently not only reminds you who you are, but also prepares you for the next time the dragon of fear begins to whisper or shout the old lies over you again.

ACTIVATE THE WAY OF THE DRAGON SLAYER

DEFINE THE DRAGON

The fear of inadequacy, self-hatred, and disqualification is the most pervasive dragon every man faces. Almost as soon as we become self-aware, and often before, the accuser lures and intimidates us into the cultivation of a false self based on the insecure basis of our performance, possessions, personality, or some other trait. It's like being trapped in a carnival funhouse of distorted mirrors—none of the faces looking back at us are the real us, but we think they are, which is terrifying. Defeating this dragon requires us to search and find the mirror who can show us who we truly are, and that is only found by discovering who our Father says we are.

POINTS OF ATTACK

These beliefs, behaviors, and conditions keep us fueled by and trapped in this fear:

- Toxic self-talk—you partner with the Accuser to diminish yourself.
- Shame and self-punishment—after a mistake or failure, you accept a lowering in your sense of worth.

- Isolation—you decide to over-value your own perspective and judgment and push others away.
- Ignorance—you fail to gather input or feedback from God and loving fathers, brothers, and friends, leading to a lack of knowledge.
- Depression—you swim in anxiety due to your insecurities, thus depleting you of energy

Which of these areas feel like the most obvious area of attack in your life right now? How have you invited brothers in to fight with you?

LESSONS LEARNED

"You're my son, (put your name here), and I love you. You're my boy, and I love you. I loved you from the first minute that I saw you, and that will never change. (Your name), you're my boy. You're amazing. I love you. I am proud of you. I love you, son. Know that inside your heart. . . Don't carry this around anymore." (Scene from *The Adam Project*)

Can you hear your Father saying these words to you? Don't stop reading that until you believe it. Ask for prayer if you need it. This is your true identity!

THE SWORD

> "Teacher, which is the great commandment in the law?" Jesus said to him, "'You shall love the LORD your God with all your heart, with all your soul, and with all your mind.' This is the first and great commandment. And the second is like it: You shall love your neighbor as yourself.' On these two commandments hang all the Law and the Prophets." (Matthew 22:36-40)

"So husbands ought to love their own wives as their own bodies; he who loves his wife loves himself. For no one ever hated his own flesh, but nourishes and cherishes it, just as the Lord does the church." (Ephesians 5:28-29)

"He who [willfully] separates himself [from God and man] seeks his own desire, He quarrels against all sound wisdom. A [closed-minded] fool does not delight in understanding, But only in revealing his personal opinions [unwittingly displaying his self-indulgence and his stupidity]." (Proverb 18:1-2 AMP)

"Therefore there is now no condemnation [no guilty verdict, no punishment] for those who are in Christ Jesus [who believe in Him as personal Lord and Savior]. For the law of the Spirit of life [which is] in Christ Jesus [the law of our new being] has set you free from the law of sin and of death." (Romans 8:1-2)

HOW TO SLAY

1. Reflect. Self-awareness is key! Take a DISC assessment, Strengthsfinder, or whatever assessment tool you find that helps and learn about how you are wired, designed, and positioned to represent Jesus to others. Stop applying your weaknesses to the strengths of other people.

a. What is your DISC result?

b. What are your top ten strengths and bottom five in the Strengthsfinder assessment?

c. Let the men you are running with see these results and learn who they are as well.

2. Connect. Who do you surround yourself with? Do your friends know who you really are and call you back to your identity when you deviate from it? Commit your life, love, and service to other men who are on a similar journey of growth and maturity, who you respect and trust.
3. Adjust. Create a list of declarations from the "aha" moments in your self-discovery and healing journey. Write them down, post them on your mirror or places you see regularly, speak them aloud, and meditate on them. Here are some I have found effective for me and others:

a. My God is powerful!

b. My God is with me!

c. My God has called me!

d. My God works all things together for my good

e. I slay every day!

CHAPTER 4
MAN WITH WOMAN

Sheri and I got saved and married in a few whirlwind months at age twenty-two. The honeymoon wore off in seconds, and only sheer grace and some kind of stubbornness in both of us—a rebellion against our often-divorced-and-remarried parents—kept us from throwing in the towel. After twelve-plus years of cycling through failure after failure as we struggled to create, maintain, and protect our connection, however, we didn't have high levels of hope and vision that we were ever going to crack the code on how to have a happy marriage. We were pretty much chronically disconnected, and our brief interludes of connection were always too fragile to endure beyond the next disagreement or disappointment.

By that point it was the late 1990s, we had three kids, I had finished a master's degree, and I had just transitioned from my nine-year career in social work to become the Associate Pastor at Bill Johnson's church in Weaverville, California. We began to hear about a new prophetic inner healing model called "Sozo" that was providing a "kinder and gentler" form of deliverance for people trying to get free of past trauma, addictions, and demonic oppression. We really had no idea what it was or what to expect, but when a couple of ladies offered this ministry to our church, Sheri was among the first to sign up for a session.

I couldn't believe this was going to happen. If anyone needed to be healed from their past traumas, it was Sheri. She had been raised in an MMA-style home with six brothers and two parents who could hardly stand each other. They'd both been married twice before and were just hanging on to this marriage by sheer will. Sheri learned to fight for everything she got and knew it was her job to "protect herself at all times." Meanwhile, I was the "good guy" in our marriage. I was the one bending over backwards to accommodate her every whim and mood. I was the one in charge of her happiness and the peace and calm of our home. I was the one who had no needs and didn't matter as much as she did. The idea that she was willing to try and figure out what was wrong with her and fix it felt like a miracle! I thought this might be the salvation of our marriage.

At last, the day of Sheri's Sozo appointment arrived. The session lasted over two hours. She got home late in the evening and didn't volunteer any information about how it had gone. The next afternoon when I asked her how it went, she just said, "It was good." This was an unusually minimal amount of communication on her part, so I pressed her for more details. Little did I know that I had just invited a blow to the head from a two-by-four.

She began by sharing that the Lord had shown her many things she did not realize about her past, her view of herself, her relationship with Him, and who He wanted to be in her life. In particular, He showed her that she'd never felt protected.

Certainly not! I thought. *You were raised by wolves!* I supposed that the next thing she would tell me was who she had spent time forgiving.

"He showed me that I've never felt protected by you."

What? Unfortunately, I didn't really hear anything she said after that, because I was too preoccupied feeling shocked, triggered, and pissed. *You never felt protected by me! How in the world did I end up in your Sozo? You were supposed to get healed up from what your family did to you! What is going on? I am the victim here! I cannot believe that this has been turned around and now I am to blame!*

I spent the remainder of the afternoon sulking and wondering why the Lord had failed to show Sheri the real problem. Finally, He interrupted my pity party and asked, "Did you hear what I said?"

"Yes, I heard what she said."

"Did you hear what I said?" He repeated.

"Yes, I heard what she said."

Finally, it dawned on me. I had never once thought about protecting Sheri. She was the fighter. She was the one who got her way by being angry, demanding, and aggressive. Who protects the aggressor? Who protects the T-Rex in *Jurassic Park*?

As soon as I realized this, another thought occurred to me. *Maybe she acts so desperate and hostile* because *she doesn't feel protected by me.* In an instant, this thought opened up a completely different perspective on my wife. Scene after scene flooded my memory, and this time I saw her behavior from a totally new angle. She wasn't angry. She was hurt and scared. She was acting like a wounded animal. It wasn't power she was demonstrating when she lashed out, it was panic.

It didn't take long for my suspicion to become a certainty. I did not nor had I ever protected my wife. In fact, I had spent twelve years protecting myself and everyone around her instead of having one thought to protect her. This meant I wasn't the kind, good, long-suffering husband I thought I was. I was a passive, lying coward! Wow! No wonder she didn't trust me. I had failed at the most primary level of my role as a husband: Protector.

This was a shattering revelation about my part in our marriage difficulties. It was also the most helpful information I'd ever received. I finally saw the problem. But what was I going to do? I was still afraid of her anger. I was still afraid of being hurt by her words and rejection. I had no skills to deal with a woman's anger. I was raised by a single mom who was almost never angry. She attracted angry men and I learned to become a small target. Now I was thirty-four years old and had no idea how to tackle this problem.

But that wasn't entirely true, I realized. I had spent nine years as a social worker in group homes and domestic violence intervention courses practicing how to disarm aggressive people and be an assertive leader in chaotic situations. I had just never used any of those tools in my marriage. Curious, I decided to start experimenting with what I had learned about how to lower anxiety and create a safe place to communicate and connect. To my astonishment, it worked. There was a learning curve, of course—I didn't always hit the target. But little by little, I started to make Sheri feel safe. We started to feel connected, and we learned how to stay connected. By our fifteenth anniversary, we looked at each other and couldn't believe it. We were happy. We were enjoying each other. We had actually turned our marriage around.

This breakthrough and transformation didn't just save our marriage, however. It became fruit that we started passing out to everyone we met. Without that fundamental tectonic plate shift of Sheri being honest with me and me being willing to move into my role as her protector, we wouldn't have a ministry—no Loving on Purpose, no books, no KYLO Show, no Dragon Slayers.

Of course, moving into that role forced me to do battle with a dragon—the fear of rejection, disconnection, and betrayal. The irony was that I had never really experienced this fear before I married Sheri. It became immediately clear that I had married my opposite in every way. Most of us do, probably because deep down we know they have something we need, though we don't yet appreciate that getting it will require us to confront our deepest weaknesses, grow, and change. It took me twelve-plus years to finally realize that my wife was not, in fact, the dragon, but the loud and insistent invitation I needed to face the real dragon of my own fear so I could become the powerful protector I longed to be in my core.

THE WAY OF THE DRAGON SLAYER

The Nature of the Dragon:
The Fear of Rejection, Disconnection, and Betrayal

The relationship between a man and his wife is his most important relationship after his relationship with God and himself. The Bible's origin story of marriage not only establishes this as the relational order of creation—it also reveals that God required the man to experience his *need* for a wife before He brought her to him. The first thing God called "not good" was a lonely man, a man without a "helpful opposite" to be his companion, friend, partner, and lover, and He allowed the man to taste this loneliness before assuaging it with Eve's arrival. Both man and woman were designed to experience a unique completion and empowerment to be themselves and fulfill their purpose in partnership with each other.

However, this very need for the woman created a paradox of vulnerability for the man. He was vulnerable without the woman—vulnerable to loneliness, frustration, and lack of purpose and legacy. Yet he was also vulnerable with her—vulnerable to the pain of her rejection, disconnection, and betrayal. It was this paradox that created the fundamental challenge and problem for the man to solve. To stay in this relationship and experience the fulfillment of his need, he had to figure out how to protect his wife and their connection while remaining vulnerable. He had to work to protect her from himself by refusing to protect himself from her.

As long as the man operated in the posture of a protector, he positioned himself to receive the greatest gift a woman can offer a man, which is her vulnerability, both physical and emotional. Winning the heart and trust of a woman is among the highest validations of manhood, because this is who we were designed to be—protectors of feminine vulnerability. Codes of honor and chivalry have always recognized that men ought to protect not only their wives, but all women. Our strength as men is to cherish and nourish them, not to exploit, oppress, or objectify them.

It is precisely for that reason that our enemy plotted to steal our strength by deceiving the woman and using her to entice the man to sin. Apparently he knew that the way to get to Adam was through Eve. As many Bible scholars have pointed out, Adam's first failure was not eating the fruit of the forbidden tree—it was standing passively by as the serpent deceived his wife and then going along with her as they took the fruit. The man did absolutely nothing to protect his wife, their marriage, and the garden from the enemy. Then, instead of repenting when he realized what he had done, he doubled down and accused his wife (and by extension, God—"this woman *You* gave me") of being the enemy. He became the one to reject her, disconnect from her, and betray her. God's pronouncement to Eve—"Your desire will be for your husband, and he will rule over you"—was a description of how things would be because the man now believed his job was protecting himself *from* her instead of protecting her. Instead of a powerful, life-giving partnership, man's relationship with the woman became one of control, domination, and exploitation—all thanks to the fear of rejection, disconnection, and betrayal that was now driving him.

THE WAY OF THE DRAGON SLAYER

Riding the Dragon: Subtle Predators

In Western culture today there is a full-on assault in effect toward the role of protector for men. We see it in the many ways our educational system emasculates our boys and defames women in the name of so-called "feminism," and in the way our entertainment, music, and porn industries encourage outright predatory exploitation of women. We see it on the extreme poles of our culture war, where on one end we have men who are so committed to deconstructing gender that they can't define what a woman is, and on the other end we have the "manosphere" embracing more or less a religious fundamentalist view that women should be second-class, submissive, and the property of men. We are raising an entire generation of men who believe women don't want their protection, that acting predatory towards women is acceptable, or that they don't have what it takes to protect anyone but themselves.

Given the current cultural landscape, it's easy to find men who are either egregiously aggressive dragon riders in their relationship with women—seducers, misogynists, wife beaters, rapists—or extremely passive—young men who have destroyed their ability to connect with a woman and retreat from life and relationships. But some of the most troubling dragon riders are those who have learned to hide in plain sight as quiet, unassuming, even gentle and accommodating Christian men.

I once knew a man named George who was one of these subtle, passive-aggressive dragon riders. Somehow, George managed to conceal his dragon-riding tendencies from his wife Lindsay before they were married. Almost immediately after the wedding, however, he began to approach her in ways that made her feel violated, intimidated, and controlled. Over and over, he communicated that he had no respect for her body, time, energy, or space. Despite Lindsay sending many cues, from body language to directly confronting the behavior and asking him to stop, he seemed incapable of getting the message that he needed to adjust his behavior. Finally, she asked him to leave. At first it was just the bedroom. When he continued to violate her boundaries, she asked him to leave the house.

George and Lindsay came to me for counseling. I watched George flounder as he tried to figure out just what he was doing to make his wife so upset. It only took me a few minutes to see the problem as I listened to them talk about a situation. Lindsay explained that she had been in their room alone with the door shut because she'd asked George for space. George had come to the bedroom door, opened it, and asked, "Do you mind if I come in and ask a question?" For some reason, he didn't realize that he had already done both. George had used respectful words to mask a disrespectful action—coming into the room without permission—which sent the message, "You cannot keep me out of your space." Then, when Lindsay expressed her anxiety and explained that she felt violated, he acted like a victim.

I explained to George that this was a perfect example of the "Law of the Door." The door is a physical boundary that represents a spiritual and emotional boundary. There is a reason there is a door between him and Lindsay and it is shut. A loving man who is paying attention to his connection with his woman and his role will see that boundary and respect it. He will start to manage himself and his anxieties and protect her from himself when needed.

Joseph, the father of Jesus, was a great example of this kind of respectful man. We often forget that the Christmas story begins with a peculiar adult twist—Joseph's betrothed Mary became pregnant by God, or so she claimed. At first Joseph didn't believe this story and was ready to kick Mary to the curb and move on with his life. But he had a dream in which the Lord affirmed that she was telling the truth. Joe decided to believe the dream and marry the pregnant virgin. Even more impressively, "they refrained from having sex until she gave birth to her firstborn son, whom they named 'Jesus'" (Matthew 1:25 TPT). Wait—didn't he have a right to "husband privileges" with the new wife he'd dedicated his life to, especially since he was going to take a lot of heat when people found out about the "pregnant by the Holy Spirit" story? As it was, most people were going to assume that either he had been intimate with Mary before the wedding, or she had cheated on him with someone else, neither of which enhanced his reputation. If everyone assumed they were doing it anyway, he might as well indulge—it might at least dispel rumors of unfaithfulness on her part. Yet to show his great respect for both God and Mary, Joseph decided to treat her as he would treat God Himself. He recognized that there was something holy happening in Mary's space, body, time, and needs, and whether he understood or agreed or not, and no matter what anyone else thought, he was going to honor that boundary with his whole heart. Joseph was going to protect Mary from Joseph—and the rest of the world. There's a reason God chose a man with this character to protect the mother of His Son. Joseph knew how to respect the Law of the Door.

George, in contrast, refused to see that Lindsay was protecting herself from him because he wasn't protecting her from him. George didn't get a dream or an angel, but he did get his wife's voice numerous times. The disconnect and extra space she was requiring were painful for George, so he kept trying to force the gap closed and didn't understand why it wasn't closing. Instead, each violation was spiking her anxiety and making the door thicker and heavier. As a friend once told me, "Your fences need to be horse-high, pig-tight, and bull-strong." In other words, the intensity of the boundary is meant to communicate the level of threat the other person is experiencing.

I tried to explain to George that respecting the door and other boundaries Lindsay was setting would communicate to her that he was willing to protect her. If the door was shut, he shouldn't have opened it. Even if it was partially open, he should ask to enter her space. Showing respect for her boundaries would help her believe that he respected the rest of her. Sadly, despite Lindsay giving him multiple chances to change, George either could not or would not do the work to figure out what his wife needed to feel safe with him. In the end, they separated and divorced.

Along with this type of subtle aggression, there are plenty of men who are subtly passive and withdrawn in their marriages. This is the case with many Christian men who end up struggling with porn. Usually there's some kind of inciting event that creates distance or disconnection between the man and his wife—an argument, the demands of children or work, an illness, or her "moods." Instead of being self-controlled, courageous, and self-sacrificial in moving towards his wife, having the tough conversation to reconnect, getting creative in carving out time together, or finding ways to make her feel better, he decides to meet his own needs without her in a way he thinks he can control. He may even justify "taking care of himself" to lighten the burden on her.

The problem is that when a man uses porn, he enters a predatory part of his brain. He is now stalking someone for his own consumption. When he emerges from his binge, he no longer can view himself as a safe place, a champion of women, or a protective father. He has violated himself with his own appetites and disqualified himself as an authorized protector, which ultimately produces shame. Shame is the pain we feel when we have wounded our identity by not living up to who we were created to be. Sadly, instead of seeking the path of confession, repentance, forgiveness, and reconciliation with their true selves, God, and their wife, most men spend years trapped in the bondage of protecting a secret life that completely betrays these relationships. And thanks to the nature of addiction, he can't be satisfied with the occasional indulgence. He needs increasing amounts with increasing intensity to satisfy his urges. What began as a few stolen moments online becomes a debris field of broken hearts, broken trust, and often a broken marriage and family.

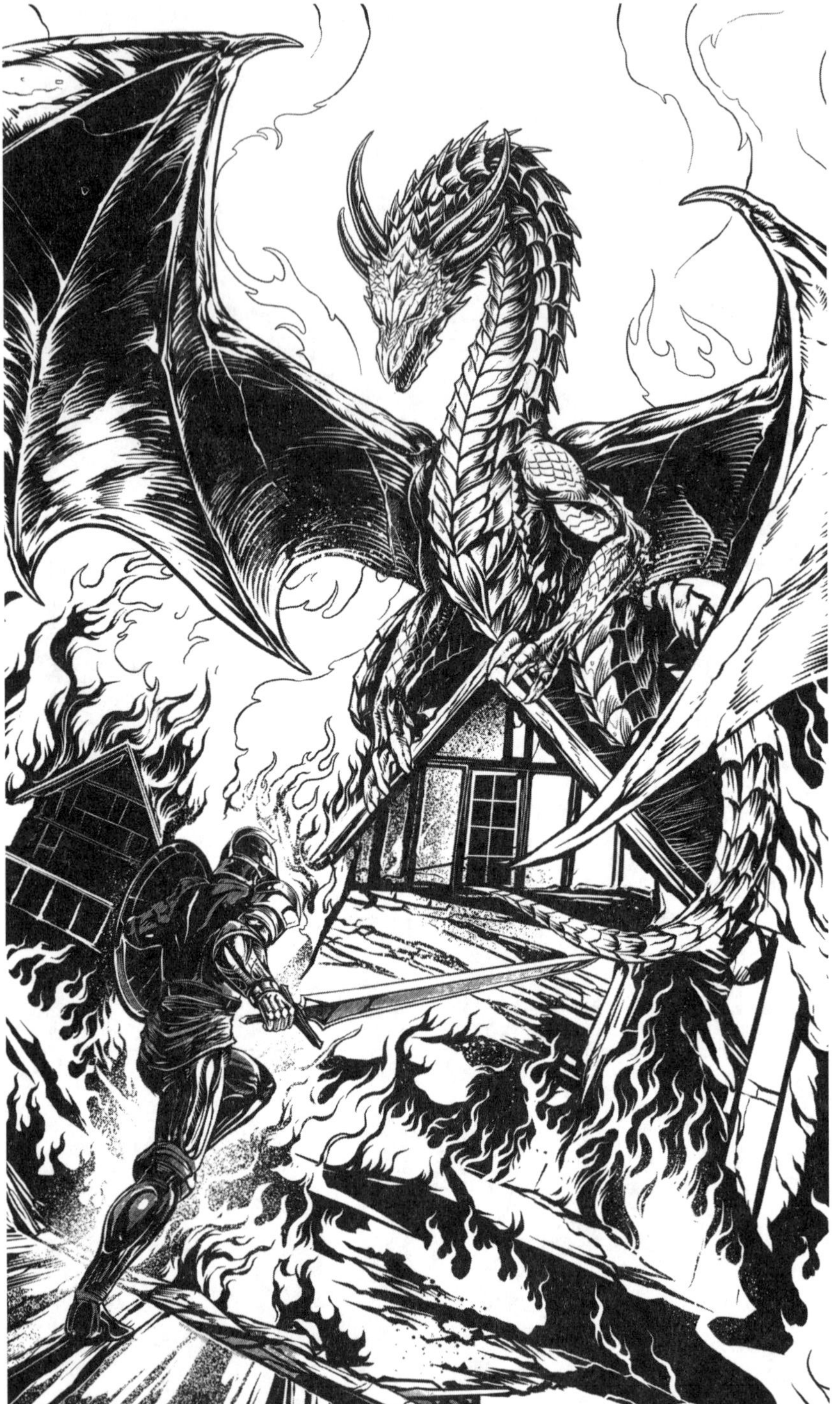

Facing the Dragon: The Sexy Butler

A few years back I hosted a bachelor party for a young man, Brian, whose wedding I was going to perform the next day. After dinner, I invited him and his groomsmen out to our fire pit. Nervous laughter, honeymoon jokes, and campfire smoke rose in the air as the beautiful summer evening faded into darkness around us. Brian, who I'd come to know as a strong, quiet type, was sitting back and enjoying the lively conversation but not really engaging in it. I could see that he was pondering something, and sure enough, during a brief lull in the banter he looked at me and asked, "Danny, what advice would you give me going into my new marriage?"

The atmosphere immediately settled as all the young men turned their fire-lit faces in my direction.

I said, "Make it your goal to be a sexy butler for the first twelve months."

Everyone smiled. One of the guys joked that he liked the "sexy" part but wasn't quite sure about the "butler" part.

"Could you explain?" Brian asked.

"Sure," I responded. "If all goes well, you two are going to be like a couple of rabbits for a while. There won't be a room in the house where you can't find your 'sexy.' But the 'butler' part is taking the role of a servant, and I think that's where most young men fail. We get tricked into believing that our identity is wrapped up in keeping the woman from controlling us. We need her validation so much, but we're scared to be that vulnerable with her. So we set out to conquer our woman's voice. We listen less to what she needs and more to what we need. Quickly, competition enters the relationship over whose needs are the most important. Set your intention in the beginning of your marriage to conquer yourself and your selfish posturing. Make it your goal to remove the competition. Don't be the guy who undermines the message he convincingly gave his wife early on that she was his top priority. If you spend the first twelve months making yourself second to her, you will accomplish what many men struggle to achieve in fifteen years of marriage."

Now I really had the guys' attention. I could see by the concerned looks on their faces that these young men were trying to get their heads around the idea that they would willingly lose the competition game just to secure the connection. Sensing that they wanted more convincing, I continued.

"Remember the guy, Westley, in the movie *The Princess Bride*? Whenever Buttercup asked him to do anything, he would answer, 'As you wish.' She even talked down to him, calling him 'farm boy' and ordering him around, and each time he disarmed her with another, 'As you wish.' No man had shown her respect or devotion like this, and before long, he had won hers in return. He became the hero in their story by first being a servant in her heart. If you spend the first twelve months as her sexy butler, you will accomplish two vital pieces of a healthy, thriving marriage. One, you will learn to cherish and nourish her with the strength of your love, honor, and covenant. And two, you will earn a higher identity in the marriage—that of a self-conqueror, not a wife-conqueror."

I allowed the group to ponder this while I added wood to the fire. Then one of the groomsmen asked what they were all wondering.

"But what about us? When do we get to be served?"

This is what the fear of rejection, disconnection, and betrayal often sounds like. It's the fear that our deepest relational needs with a woman won't be met. When this fear triggers our self-preservation and we allow it to make us more focused on ourselves than on our woman, we introduce the competitive control dance into the relationship.

We only slay this dragon by taking the role of a humble servant. Yes, she also is called to serve in the relationship. But as men, we are called to lead and initiate in setting the bar high for sacrificial love in the relationship without waiting to be served. This is why Paul instructed, "Husbands, love your wives, as Christ loved the church and gave himself up for her" (Ephesians 5:25 ESV). In the same way Jesus served us, we must serve our wife without the intention of creating an obligation for her to do something to benefit us in return. One of the classic tests for a sexy butler is to finish a day of serving well and crawl into bed knowing you hit the mark sending messages of love to your wife, and instead of getting your "payday," she tells you she's tired and just wants to go to sleep. What you do in that moment reveals if all your selfless acts were genuine. Selfless acts are void of the expectation of payment. They are not passive aggressive methods to put your woman in your debt. Our relationships become transactional when we stray away from selfless acts. Service becomes part of our character only through repetitive practice. We strengthen our covenants with service, sacrifice, and selfless acts.

I went on to say to these young men, "By the time you get through your first year serving her well, you will have a woman who knows you, believes you, and feels protected by you. You will be a man who nourishes his woman, a man she feels connected to. Ask her for anything and she will find a way to serve you well. So be the guy who has 'What about me?' in a rear-naked choke hold! Be famous for your selfless acts that nourish her."

THE WAY OF THE DRAGON SLAYER

The Way of the Dragon Slayer: Learning Her Needs

My friend Christian Zamora has been part of the Loving on Purpose team for eight years now, and in that time we've walked together through a number of challenging situations, both personal and professional. Each time, I've seen him navigate difficulties as a man of courage, faithfulness, and sacrificial love—for us, and especially for his family.

Recently, the Zamora family experienced a season of loss and grief when his wife Bre suffered a miscarriage. After years of thinking they were done having children, God opened their hearts to the possibility of having one more, and they were thrilled when Bre discovered she was pregnant. A few months later, they learned they were having a girl, and even picked out a name for her—Mila Rose. Christian, who had thus far been a boy dad, began to imagine a life celebrating princess parties, attending father-daughter dances, fending off would-be boyfriends, and walking his little girl down the aisle one day. But then Bre began experiencing signs that something wasn't right with the pregnancy. Every time she brought this up with Christian, however, he either dismissed her concerns or countered them with positivity, assuring her everything would be fine and declaring promises from Scripture full of hope for the future.

This continued until a question he definitely knew was not his own entered his mind during his morning prayers: *What would you do if your wife had a miscarriage?* After trying to rebuke, cast out, and quote Scripture at this persistent thought, he finally realized it was the Lord. As soon as he decided to consider this possibility head on, he broke down "ugly" crying with deep grief. It felt as though God was allowing him to feel the pain He would feel over such an event. As he wept, he became aware that Bre had been walking around with this looming sorrow on her mind. Instead of recognizing that she was scared and needed help figuring out what was going on in her body, he had been sending the message that he didn't care about her feelings and was the only one "living by faith" in the situation—all because he had been too afraid to face the reality that something was actually wrong.

After dropping their boys off at school later that morning, he sat down with Bre and repented for not listening to her or protecting her heart as she wrestled with the fear of losing their baby. They agreed to stay hopeful but also scheduled an ultrasound appointment that afternoon to hear the baby's heartbeat and get the reassurance they needed. A few hours later, sitting in the exam room, the doctor pointed to the screen and gave them the terrible news: "Do you see that black space right there? That's where we should see your baby's heartbeat. You've had a miscarriage."

Within moments, Christian watched the deep sorrow that had ripped through him that morning descend on his wife. Despite feeling like his own heart had just stopped beating, the tears he had already shed in anticipation of this moment prepared him to hold Bre and comfort her as her tears began to flow. Next came the heavy task of breaking the news to their two young sons, close family, and friends—followed by the excruciating process of Bre going into labor to deliver the body of their baby girl, which Christian was forced to watch through a glass wall in the ER due to the COVID protocols in the hospital at the time.

As they entered the season of grieving this loss as a family, Christian found that his encounter with the Lord the morning of the miscarriage had prepared him to process his own sadness while continuing to comfort his wife and lead his two boys through wrestling with the difficult question of why God would allow their baby sister to die. He explained to them that God was just as brokenhearted as they were, that He hadn't wanted this to happen, that death was part of living in a fallen world, and that Mila was now with Jesus and God still had good plans for their family. They were going to continue to trust and praise Him even through this painful loss.

The happy ending to this story is that God not only healed Christian and Bre's hearts—He gave them the desire and willingness to try again for another child. This time around, each stage of the journey—trying to get pregnant, getting a positive result, learning they were going to have a boy, and facing complications that included near-preeclampsia and a c-section delivery—required another level of courage and faith from them both. Bre's fears and concerns were understandably amplified, but Christian stayed present with her through the process, listening and responding to what she was feeling and needing. A little over a year after the miscarriage, they welcomed a healthy baby boy, Justus James, marveling not only at this blessing from God, but at how they had emerged from the season of their greatest loss as a couple feeling more deeply connected than ever.

The thing I love about this story was the way the Lord guided Christian into becoming the protector his wife needed. He helped him face the threat barrelling toward their family—loss and grief—ahead of time so he could take care of Bre's heart as they endured it together. In the process, He equipped him to listen to, understand, and serve his wife and meet her needs even more effectively, thus deepening their bond. So many couples end up disconnected after experiencing the loss of a child, because they didn't know how to protect their connection and move toward each other in the midst of pain. While protecting connection in marriage is the responsibility of both husband and wife, it makes a huge difference when the man takes the lead by stepping into his role as a protector and connector. And the primary way he does this is by putting his wife's needs before his own.

Men and women were designed to come into a marriage relationship with different, yet complementary needs, because this is what produces life and growth. Carl Jung wrote, "The meeting of two personalities is like the contact of two chemical substances; if there is any reaction, both will be transformed." When we consider men and women, it's logical to conclude that our Creator had reaction and transformation in mind when He fashioned us. And He called it "very good"! It's good that we're different and that our opposites attract. It's good that women's needs aren't the same as men's needs in a relationship. It implies that we have to work, expand, contribute, and grow to nourish the connection.

Relational health between a woman and man is a cycle of supply and demand, like most things in nature. There is a supply of sunshine and a demand for photosynthesis. There is a supply of water underground and a demand for it by the roots of the forest. These cycles are in harmony with each other and make a way for each element of nature to form vital relationships that cause them to thrive through communicating and meeting very different needs.

The most compelling demand a man brings to a relationship with a woman is the need to breed. As animalistic as this sounds, it's true. Masculine energy is procreative. The guy is designed to be the one most responsible for the continuance of the species. It's not a curse or a blemish in the design of a man any more than the front and rear wing of a Formula 1 race car is problematic. With design comes a pattern of predictable function. We've been created to survive, so we are going to!

For women, the compelling demand is emotional connection. They need to feel seen, known, and cherished on the level of their heart and soul. Being "emotional" is not a curse or blemish of her design either. It speaks to her orientation to care about the other dimensions of our humanness beyond the physical.

While men, in a general sense, are wired for sexual, physical, and constructive behaviors, they still have the ability to tap into the feminine energy of their humanity, just as a woman can relate to and appreciate masculine energy. This is critical, because if either gender had no ability to appreciate what the other needed, it would be extremely difficult for them to care about meeting those needs. Instead, we have what I call the "90/10" dynamic. It's the idea that 90 percent of a man's motivation in a relationship is sexual and 10 percent is emotional, while 90 percent of the woman's motivation is emotional and 10 percent is sexual. It is this 10 percent that each of them can tap into to understand what the other person needs and care about supplying it. When a woman's need for connection and emotional nourishment finds a supply, she is open to receive what the man brings to the relationship. A man is willing to court, romance, or nurture her because he knows that this is what she needs to reciprocate by engaging in the sexual side of their relationship. When both man and woman are fulfilling the integrity of their 90 percent towards each other and meeting the sexual and emotional needs in the relationship, we have the dynamic of a combustion engine in peak performance firing on all cylinders!

I realize that these ratios are generalizations and that shelves of books have been written about the differences and needs of men and women. My goal here is not to cover all of that, but to make the point that serving a woman in a relationship requires us to understand that what she needs us to be and do for her is different from what we need her to be and do for us. If we want to succeed in our role as a "sexy butler" and become the protector, provider, and connector of our wife's heart, then we need to become a student of her needs.

Before Sheri called me up as a protector, I really wasn't cued into this aspect of serving her well. I realized that she had needs and they were different from mine, but I really didn't want to do the work to understand her deeply. I just kept searching for a magical remote that had a "make Sheri happy" button on it. When she finally told me exactly what she needed, something finally clicked in me that I had been going about things the wrong way.

My book *Keep Your Love On* captures the most important keys I discovered to becoming the protector of Sheri's heart. Some years after the book came out, I consolidated these principles into what I called The KYLO 5. Mastering these will not only make you a better husband, but a better man in all your relationships. Here they are:

1. Be powerful.

Being powerful is all about managing ourselves—our emotions, beliefs, thoughts, choices, and behavior—instead of other people. Before Sheri told me she didn't feel protected by me, I thought it was my job to calm her down and make everything better. But I realized I wasn't doing this to serve her—I was doing it to protect myself from her. I was trying to manipulate her so that I could find a safe place for me and the kids. I worked my butt off trying to control her and never thought of controlling the person I did have control over—myself. I began to control myself and choose my responses to her fear, pain, and powerlessness.

2. Choose love over fear.

Love and fear are two opposing spiritual forces that motivate completely contrary mindsets, perspective, goals, logic, and behavior. The goal of love in a relationship is always a safe heart-to-heart connection, while fear pursues a safe controllable distance. Love embraces vulnerability, while fear armors up. Love leads to self-sacrifice; fear leads to self-preservation. We get to choose which spirit we will align ourselves and partner with in our relationship.

The biggest thing I noticed when I began to choose to partner with the spirit of love is how it changed my filter for perceiving Sheri's behavior. Looking at her through a filter of fear, I never saw her fear, pain, or powerlessness when she talked. All I saw was anger, and I reacted to it by taking it personally, acting like a victim, and making myself a small target. Everything about the conversation changed when I saw her with my love "on." Instead of running away from her rage, I began moving toward her in her pain.

3. Keep connection as the goal.

Getting scared, hurt, or triggered in relationships is going to happen. But when we allow these experiences to get us to turn our love off, partner with fear, and change our goal in the relationship, then *we* are the problem. The reason Sheri and I kept getting disconnected, I realized, was because I abandoned the goal of connection every time I got scared or hurt and started pursuing a safe distance, all while blaming her for the disconnection. I had to own that no one was to blame for me turning my love off toward my wife but me. To train myself to respond differently, I started declaring in my heart and mind, "My goal with you is connection." The first time I said this to Sheri in the middle of an argument, the effect was remarkable. The level of anxiety and tension in the conversation immediately dropped, and we were able to shift in a much more productive direction. This simple statement is an anxiety killer!

4. Practice respectful communication.

One of the things that stunned me as I began to learn to protect Sheri's heart is something that is probably true of more of us men than we'd like to admit. I had never really listened to my wife. I would be silent in the face of her anger and then rage myself, spilling all the anxiety I was feeling right back into the conversation. It's a classic problem in high-stakes conversations. Instead of listening, we simply wait for the other person to finish speaking while building out our defense in our minds. This never goes anywhere productive, because it is rooted in the fundamental of disrespect: "I have no value for your thoughts, feelings, and needs."

Once I stopped focusing on protecting myself, I was able to listen with curiosity and the goal of understanding her. I began to practice reflective listening, responding with, "Is this what you are saying/feeling?" and actually collaborating with her in getting the vital information inside her out where we could both see and understand it. Only after I showed her that I had listened to her did I tell her about me.

It takes courage and vulnerability to serve our wife by listening to her first in a conversation. But here's what I learned. Listening first actually gives us an advantage in the conversation. It means that we end up being the ones with all the information—her thoughts, feelings, and needs, and ours. This means we are the ones most likely to see the solution to whatever it is she may be needing. And when we hit the target meeting her needs, guess what? We become the sexiest of butlers in her eyes. This is why the sexy butler is committed to being the best listener in the relationship. He knows the first one to listen well wins, and it's going to be him.

Of course, having all the information can only happen because we have also done our homework to figure out what we think, feel, and need. The classic stereotype is that most men are so disconnected from their own hearts that they don't even know what's rattling around inside them, much less have the words to communicate it. But the sexy butler understands that to have a heart-to-heart connection with his woman, he needs to be able to show her his heart. He is courageous to enter the vulnerability with her.

I should mention that the men in my life played a key role in my journey of learning to practice this kind of "brave communication" with Sheri. In moments of frustration or discouragement, I would ask them, "What am I doing wrong?" Every time, they all said the same thing: "Humble yourself." At first, I could not figure out what that meant besides becoming passive. Then I put it together that humility in relationships is about understanding how other people experience us, which we can only do by making it a goal to learn this information. When I realized that "humble yourself" meant "let your wife give you feedback," it shifted me toward the serving posture I needed to be taking in our conversations. Like most men, I had been instinctively avoiding this position of vulnerability in my marriage, and I needed other men, brothers and fathers, to call me to step into it.

5. Honor healthy boundaries.

A healthy relationship has lines of demarcation. It's my job to control me, and your job to control you. It's my job to tell you about me, and your job to tell me about you. The moment either of us steps in to manage the other person's half of the relationship, we have introduced disrespect to our connection. The moment we get controlling or hurtful or scary in a conversation, we are directly attacking our connection. These are the moments where we need to introduce a boundary—not to protect us from one another, but to protect our connection.

In my relationship with Sheri, one of the boundaries I started learning was how to start over in a conversation when it started to become disrespectful rather than either escalating it or shutting down and disengaging. Typically, whatever we were arguing over was just the surface issue. The deeper problem was that we had lost the connection somewhere, and that's why we were struggling to agree on something relatively inconsequential. If one or both of us stopped listening, that was a good time to stop talking. If either became disrespectful, accusatory, or punishing, then the other would say, "I'd be happy to continue this conversation if it's respectful." We learned to put the conversation down and refocus on repairing our connection before continuing to discuss the issue we were clashing over.

At this point in our forty years together, we've turned the KYLO 5 into an art form, and I can't remember the last time we were disconnected. We went from living mostly disconnected to living in a connection that has only continued to grow stronger with each passing year. Everything changed when Sheri was vulnerable enough to tell me she needed me to be her protector, and I was willing to go find the repentance, tools, and courage I needed to meet that need. If I can do it, so can you!

ACTIVATE THE WAY OF THE DRAGON SLAYER

DEFINE THE DRAGON

The fear of rejection, disconnection, and betrayal arises in our relationship with women, and especially in marriage, because of the way this relationship uniquely calls on our role as protectors, providers, and connectors. Our gendered needs are part of our complementary design, but because needs are areas of vulnerability, the temptation is to bring in tools of self-protection and control instead of choosing to lead in serving, protecting, and providing for the one who has what we need. We must slay this fear if we hope to become a man who can protect and ultimately be nourished by the heart of a woman.

POINTS OF ATTACK

These beliefs, behaviors, and conditions keep us fueled by and trapped in this fear:

- Self-gratification—I move from protector to predator.
- Self-preservation—I change the goal from intimate connection to distance.

- Self-pity—I turn the focus to "What about me?"
- Self-justification—I have a great reason for my destructive behavior.
- Pride—I refuse to be corrected or accountable.

Which of these areas feel like the most obvious area of attack in your life right now? How have you invited brothers in to fight with you?

LESSONS LEARNED

- The cloak of humility marks me as a target of God's grace.
- I am here to serve, not be served.
- Feminine vulnerability needs my masculine protection.
- Boys need men to teach them how to treat women.

THE SWORD

> Therefore humble yourselves under the mighty hand of God, that He may exalt you in due time, casting all your care upon Him, for He cares for you. Be sober, be vigilant; because your adversary the devil walks about like a roaring lion, seeking whom he may devour. Resist him, steadfast in the faith, knowing that the same sufferings are experienced by your brotherhood in the world. (1 Peter 5:6-9)

> Jesus, knowing their thoughts, called them to his side and said, "Kings and those with great authority in this world rule oppressively over their subjects, like tyrants. But this is not your calling. You will lead by a completely different model. The

greatest one among you will live as the one who is called to serve others, because the greatest honor and authority is reserved for the one with the heart of a servant. For even the Son of Man did not come expecting to be served by everyone, but to serve everyone, and to give his life in exchange for the salvation of many." (Matthew 20:25-28 TPT)

The proverbs of Solomon the son of David, king of Israel:
To know wisdom and instruction,
To perceive the words of understanding,
To receive the instruction of wisdom,
Justice, judgment, and equity;
To give prudence to the simple,
To the young man knowledge and discretion—
A wise man will hear and increase learning,
And a man of understanding will attain wise counsel,
To understand a proverb and an enigma,
The words of the wise and their riddles.
The fear of the LORD is the beginning of knowledge,
But fools despise wisdom and instruction. (Proverbs 1:1-7)

HOW TO SLAY

1. Reflect: A man with a wife, a brother with a sister, a father with a daughter or any other concoction or combination stirs the masculine heart to protect, provide and connect. Take a moment and

think about how each of these roles play out in your life currently.

    a. How do you protect women?

    b. How do you provide for them?

    c. How do you connect with a woman?

2. Connect.

    a. Ask the woman/women in your life:

        i. "How are you experiencing me?" (She tells you about her, not about you.)

ii. "What do you need to feel from me going forward?" (Tell me what you need to feel, not what you want me to do.)

iii. "Do I have any messes to clean up?" (Have I hurt, scared, or left you feeling powerless or sad?)

iv. Be prepared to listen well and be grateful for what you learn. "Thank you for telling me the truth and helping me see you" is a great response!

e. Instead of venting, share any marriage struggles with your brothers and invite them to ask good questions or offer advice to help support you and your marriage.

3. Adjust. Own your stuff, clean up your messes and lead in love and connection.

CHAPTER 5

MAN WITH MAN

I'm going to introduce you to my friend Craig Moseley with a hunting story.

In October of 2016, I took my son-in-love Ben Serpell and our friend Wes Kotys on a week-long hunting trip to Kodiak Island just off the southern coast of Alaska. There we teamed up with Craig and two other friends, Shain Zumbrunnen and Phillip Ward—all native Alaskans seasoned in hunting the local (and very delicious) Sitka blacktail deer. We also chartered a boat where we could sleep safe from bears and fish for Alaskan halibut. Our mission was to return home with a rich spread of Alaska "surf and turf" to enjoy with our families.

On our first day, we divided into three pairs and set off into the wilderness. I intentionally paired Ben with Craig, who we affectionately call "the Alaskan Bear Grylls." Craig was born and raised in the Alaskan outback and regularly takes guys out on trips to explore, hunt, bond, and develop their survival skills.

"Craig, this is Ben's second hunt, and the first time he's used that 30.06 rifle," I informed him. "I have one goal for this week—I need Ben to come home alive!"

"Sure thing," Craig agreed.

At the end of the day when we rendezvoused back on the shore, Ben appeared grinning and shouldering his first buck! I couldn't have been more thrilled that he was first to get a kill.

After a most enjoyable evening during which Craig regaled us with hunting stories— including a jaw-dropping one about a grizzly bear that charged him and only went down after being plugged by eleven rounds—we headed out at sunrise the next morning, hoping the rest of us could score a buck. Sure enough, by early afternoon Phillip, Wes, and I had all returned to the shore with a buck a piece. When Craig and Ben failed to show up by the time we had loaded them onto the inflatable Zodiak, we took off, figuring they must already be back on the boat.

We were right. "Did you guys get something?" I asked after Ben and Craig had helped us hoist a couple hundred pounds of dressed deer onto the boat.

"Well," Craig began—his tone and look said he had a story to tell—"We headed up the coast line a ways, put in at a cove to the north, and started hiking. On one ridge, we saw a bear with a couple cubs off in the distance, so we kept going and got to a point where we could look down from another ridge on a nice bowl. I started glassing around (looking through binoculars) and saw a couple bucks. Then I saw a big bear on the other side of the bowl from us, about seven hundred yards away. It was locked onto us and I started getting uncomfortable at its glare. I stood up and waved my arms, hoping to spook it. Well, that didn't work. That thing started charging at us. I shot a few warning shots and it kept coming. About a hundred yards out, it stopped and stood up to look over the brush to find us. So I shot the fourth warning shot."

"At this point all I can think about is that story he told last night about the grizzly and how it took eleven hits to kill it," Ben chimed in. "He's just emptied his gun, and I have four in mine. Even if he has time to reload, that's only eight."

"I did reload," Craig continued. "And that bear started crashing through the bushes right at us. About twenty yards out, it stopped again and stood up to look for us. I said to Ben, 'If that bear takes one step in our direction, we start shooting.' Sure enough, a few seconds later it charged us. Ben shot first and hit it in the shoulder, spun it to the right. I hit it in the neck and it dropped about ten yards from us. We each unloaded one more into it and that did it."

We were all standing with our mouths wide open at this point. "Ben, are you all right, buddy?" I asked.

Ben shrugged and managed to smile.

The captain of our chartered boat, Garrett, spoke up. "Well, all I know is that I'm going to have to put some more chemicals in the septic tank after Ben got done in there!"

We all laughed, more in relief than humor. Not every man gets within ten feet of a charging grizzly and lives to tell the tale!

Later that night around the table, we all began to call out the destiny on Ben's life, likening him to David killing the bear and the lion before slaying Goliath. Even though four of us hadn't been present for it, there was something about this encounter with danger, and the courageous actions it called forth in Ben and Craig, that set the tone for the week. We continued to speak words of encouragement and strength over one another throughout the trip, and when the time came for us to return home, laden with venison from nine bucks and a few hundred pounds of halibut (including the best halibut cheek sushi I'd ever tasted), we all knew a special bond had been forged between us. To this day we've all stayed in regular contact. We are brothers joined at the heart. Also—my favorite memento of our adventure—that bear is now a rug that hangs on a wall in our house, a testament to God's favor and protection!

More than once, I've thanked God that I paired Ben with Craig on that trip—probably the one man in the world I would want someone I loved to be with when facing a Kodiak grizzly bear. Ben was grateful too. When

Craig told Ben he was impressed that Ben didn't panic and start running like other men he'd been with in similar situations, Ben said, "Well, I trusted you. And I wasn't going to leave you there alone." Ben understood that if he wanted to survive a bear, he needed to stick with the man who had already survived many.

Craig's prowess with bears is just one facet of what makes him a man you trust to lead you safely through the wilderness, however. When I got to know Craig and learned about his journey in life, I quickly understood that this was a man with a heart and calling to be a brother and father for orphaned men.

Craig himself grew up without his biological father around (he finally met the man when he was fifty-one, right before he died of cancer). Two other men raised him—the first, his mother's second husband, was an abusive alcoholic, and the second was an authoritarian rancher who adopted Craig and his two sisters after their mother moved on to another relationship and abandoned them to fend for themselves. On the positive side, both of these men modeled a strong work ethic, a manly pride in carrying their own weight, and a responsibility to be providers for their family. On the downside, neither of them had any faith or spiritual life, didn't treat the women in their life very well, and were pretty dysfunctional when it came to family relationships. In other words, they were pretty good at the "protect" and "provide" roles in the home, but not so great at the "connect" role. As a result, Craig emerged into adulthood with a drive to work hard and be self-sufficient, but with a very broken template for family relationships. He got married and started a family, but soon began to recreate the same pain in his wife's and kids' lives that he'd been dealt. He was unfaithful to his wife in their first year of marriage and imitated the abusive, authoritarian style of fathering that had been modeled for him.

Craig knew he was on a trajectory to pass down the legacy of divorce and dysfunction to his own children, but didn't have any idea how things could be different. Thankfully, Jesus apprehended him. His sister got saved and shared the gospel with him, his wife started going to church, and friends began praying for him. Soon he joined his wife at church and gave his life to the Lord. For the entire first year of his new Christian life, Craig's pastor came to their house every Saturday and discipled him in the Word, and another associate pastor mentored him. But the event that year that really began to redesign his identity and role as a man, husband, and father was a conference led by Stu Weber, author of *Tender Warrior*.

Stu introduced Craig to two ideas he had never heard before. The first was the Father's love. Unlike the men who had raised Craig, the Father was willing to sacrifice everything to connect with His sons and daughters. He wanted them to thrive spiritually, emotionally, relationally, and in every other area of life. The second idea was that men who are trying to lead and love their families with the Father's love think *generationally*. They are intentional about not passing down harmful patterns of thinking and behavior that were modeled for them, and about cultivating life-giving patterns of thinking and behavior that they can model and train in their own children. As Craig listened to Stu describing this generational mindset, it was like a revelation that caused him to see himself from a completely new vantage point. He knew the path he had been on was entirely self-focused and wasn't going anywhere good. He wanted to become a man, husband, and father who could influence generations of his family with the love of the Father.

With this goal in his sights, Craig set out to learn how to create this generational legacy. He began looking for men around him who were loving their families well. He studied Scripture, went to Bible studies and men's conferences, and then began starting his own men's Bible studies and life groups. Gradually he gathered a group of brothers around him who were equally hungry for spiritual growth and held him accountable to stay on that path. He and his wife participated in a seven-day workshop that brought radical healing to them and their marriage. He got more healing, infilling of the Holy Spirit, and revelation of the Father's heart on a ministry trip to Brazil with Randy Clark. The more he grew, the more committed to growth he became.

As Craig progressed on this journey with the Lord, his wife, his kids, and his chosen community of spiritual brothers, it was a natural step for him to get a heart for other young men he saw at work—Craig is a superintendent for a construction company—who were walking down the fatherless, broken path he had been on. Many of these guys quickly figured out that Craig was different from other bosses or authority figures in their lives—he was respectful, encouraging, and called them to a higher standard without shaming them. If they showed interest in having a more personal conversation about their lives, he let them know that he had a "bullpen" where they could switch out of work mode and have a real talk. One by one, young men started opening up to Craig and letting him speak into their lives.

Over the last twenty-plus years, Craig has become a father in the lives of dozens of young men. To this day, he consistently has eight-to-ten guys that he meets regularly for coffee to mentor and encourage. He also leads them out on expeditions into the Alaskan wilderness to get them away from their lives, initiate them into the ways of pocketknives, guns, and campfires, and kindle the honest reflection and conversations that only seem to arise when men are working together to survive the elements. He is also still dedicated to continuing to become a better husband, father, friend, and man.

Craig's life demonstrates the power men have to influence other men. Broken men shaped his childhood, but healthy men guided him onto a better path. Now whole and healthy himself, he is laying down his life to help other broken men find the path to life and wholeness. Craig's life is really what Dragon Slayers is all about!

THE WAY OF THE DRAGON SLAYER

The Nature of the Dragon:
The Fear of Competition, Covenant, and Sacrifice

Technically, the first relationship between two men in the Bible is between Adam and his firstborn son, Cain, but we really don't get any information about that father-son relationship. Instead, Genesis 4 focuses on the relationship between Cain and his brother, Abel. You're probably familiar with the famous story. Cain kills his brother. This violent act costs Adam two sons, not one, thus sabotaging their God-given mission as a family from the beginning. Not only does Cain put Abel out of commission, he then goes and builds a city and fathers a family line whose values and actions reflected the opposite of the kingdom of God. Every great tyrant, conqueror, and narcissist throughout history who has consumed and destroyed the lives of men through rebellion and revenge has walked in the path of Cain.

The key insight in this story is the way it clarifies the sins of the heart that most often beset men in their relationships with other men: shame, envy, and revenge. Cain fell short before God, and his brother didn't. Instead of working on himself, doing better, and being restored and accepted as a good man before his Creator—which God told him he was capable of doing—Cain decided to deal with the shame of his failure by taking it out on his brother. Instead of mastering his true enemy—the sin "crouching" like a predator ready to strike him—he allowed it to distort his vision and frame his brother as the enemy. Sin, which is rooted in fear, deception, and self-preservation, forced him to see Abel (and himself) through the warped lens of competition. Abel was a winner, and he was a loser. Instead of trying to play the game by the rules, Cain decided the way to win was to end the game and eliminate the competition.

The minute Cain ceased to see Abel as a brother, he ceased to behave as a brother toward him. When God asked Cain where Abel was, he answered, "I do not know; am I my brother's *keeper*?" (Genesis 4:9). The Hebrew word is the same one in Genesis 2:15, where God put Adam in the garden to "keep" it—it means to protect, watch, guard, and preserve. The answer was yes—Cain was supposed to be his brother's protector. That is what brothers are supposed to do for one another, because brothers are supposed to love one another and lay down their lives for each other. That's how it works in the family of God—the Father expects His sons to love one another in the same way He loves them, with sacrificial, covenant love. But the minute we turn from that love to fear, we begin to align with and channel the nature of the dragon, God's enemy. This is why John the apostle described Cain as being "of the evil one":

> We should not be like Cain, who was of the evil one and murdered his brother. And why did he murder him? Because his own deeds were evil and his brother's righteous . . . Everyone who hates his brother is a murderer, and you know that no murderer has eternal life abiding in him. By this we know love, that he laid down his life for us, and we ought to lay down our lives for the brothers. (1 John 3:11-12, 15-16 ESV)

The sin that ultimately mastered Cain and turned him into dragon rider wants to master us too. To experience and walk in true brotherhood with other men as we were designed, we must face this fourth dragon—the fear of competition, covenant, and sacrifice.

THE WAY OF THE DRAGON SLAYER

Riding the Dragon: Men Who Won't Commit

There are many types and aspects of male relationships where we see this dragon at work, poisoning genuine brotherhood and producing cycles of perversion, exploitation, and destruction. In the inner cities we have generations of (mostly fatherless) boys growing up in gangs, organized crime networks, and prisons. Homosexuality has pervaded our culture, creating confusion and casting a chilling effect on male friendships. Even our national politics has become less about cooperation and "fraternity" and more and more resembles *Game of Thrones*. Yet as we have seen, some of the most common and harmful styles of dragon riding in relationships are those involving passivity and isolation, and this is certainly true in the realm of men and men.

In July of 2021, *National Review* published an article titled, "American Men Suffer a Friendship Recession."[14] The article discusses the results of a survey showing that men in our culture today are cultivating fewer and fewer friendships with other men. "The percentage of men with at least six close friends fell by half since 1990, from 55 percent to 27 percent . . . Single men fare the worst. One in five American men who are unmarried and not in a romantic relationship report not having any close friends." The author mentions several factors that have contributed to this decline—lower marriage rates, lower involvement in religion, geographic mobility, and a work culture that encourages longer hours, remote work, and frequent role changes. But he also points out something revealing:

> One common explanation for why men are less able to develop and maintain close relationships is that traditional norms of masculinity make the task of building and sustaining healthy friendships more difficult. Compared to women, men

---

14 | Daniel Cox, "American Men Suffer a Friendship Recession," *National Review*, July 6, 2021, https://www.nationalreview.com/2021/07/american-men-suffer-a-friendship-recession/

feel less comfortable sharing their feelings, being vulnerable, or seeking emotional support from their friends. While there may be some truth to this, the story is more complicated. *Younger men, who are far more likely to reject traditional notions of masculinity, struggle the most with developing enduring social bonds.*

There's a common theme in all the factors I just mentioned—*a lack of commitment.* Marrying a woman, contributing to a faith community or even just a local community, and sticking with a job or company all require commitment. It's not a mistake that young men today "reject traditional notions of masculinity" and also avoid commitment. Commitment is a masculine virtue.

So many young men I meet today, even in the church, seem terrified of commitment. They are full of excuses about why they're not engaged in the pursuits of a meaningful life. Women are either too unattractive or too risky, and marriage is a bad deal for men today—that's why they aren't dating. College is a debt trap and overrated—that's why they're still living with their parents working part time while they figure out what they want to do with their life. The church is too feminized and "woke," harsh and judgmental, commercialized and heretical, you name it—that's why they won't go on Sunday morning, much less join a homegroup. They have excuses for why they're not managing their health or finances, why they don't have goals or ambitions, and why they avoid anything that feels like hard work.

When you drill down and ask guys today why they're so commitment-avoidant, they eventually admit that they're afraid of losing various things—their time, freedom, independence, comfort, safety, or self-image. And so they don't commit to anything.

How does being non-committal make you a dragon rider? Think of the dragon Smaug in *The Hobbit.* He didn't fly around torching villages and terrorizing townsfolk every day. Most of the time he was just sleeping inside his mountain, guarding his massive treasure. This is what non-committal men are like. They're hoarders.

In his book *The Men We Need*, Brant Hansen addresses the attitude that guides many of these hoarding dragon-riders: "As long as I'm not hurting someone else, what does it matter?" By way of answering this question, he tells the story of his friend Greg:

> Because he's about my age, [Greg] also grew up in an era of video games and easily accessed pornography. At some point in his college years, he could have said, "You know what? I'm going to hole up in my room and collapse inwardly. I'm going to just play and amuse myself. As long as I'm not hurting someone else, what does it matter?"
>
> Thankfully, he didn't do that. Instead, he rose to the occasion and finished college. He then got into medical school (he says he still doesn't know how he made it) and worked very hard. He's now a pediatric cardiac anesthesiologist.
>
> Greg is remarkably good at putting scared little kids to sleep and putting their parents at ease too. He has five kids of his own and a wife who respects him deeply. Because of his desire to emulate Jesus, he's spent months traveling through developing nations (often taking his family), serving in hospitals for the poorest people in the world. He's provided first-class care to some of the most desperate little patients in the world and trained more doctors to do the same . . .

So, the obvious question: If he had, in fact, collapsed inwardly and handed himself over to video games and porn, would it have "hurt" anyone? Of course, but he wouldn't have known it. We would have missed out on the man he was supposed to be.

This is not an exaggeration. Because of the choices Greg has made, many moms and dads haven't had to attend funerals for their own children.

When we men take our roles seriously, when we're at our best, those are the kinds of things that happen. Healing. Peace. Life.

And when we don't, distortion, anxiety, violence, and meaninglessness fill the gap.[15]

In the parable of the talents, the master had the harshest words for the servant who had hoarded the money entrusted to him, and ultimately called for him to be cast "into the outer darkness" (Matthew 25:30). This is how seriously God judges the man who withholds himself from others. Specifically when it comes to what men have to offer other men, and what men need from other men, the sin of withholding, hoarding, and remaining non-committal in our culture has created a devastating famine of courage, camaraderie, and honor. For this is what good male friendships do for men. As the famous proverb states, "[As] iron sharpens iron, So a man sharpens the countenance of his friend" (Proverbs 27:17). Sharpening the countenance means to develop someone's virtue and character. Just as a warrior can only

---

15 | Brant Hansen, *The Men We Need* (Grand Rapids, MI: Baker Publishing Group, 2022), Kindle Edition, 226-227.

be properly trained with a sparring partner, so a man can only really learn to protect, provide, and connect with other men who challenge him, test him, encourage him, and call him higher.

Sadly, most of the isolated men who struggle to commit fail to realize that whatever they might lose through commitment pales in comparison to what they are already losing by avoiding it. They are forfeiting the very thing that has the power to turn them from a man who is weak, dull, useless, and lacking in character to a man who is strong, sharp, effective, and virtuous.

THE WAY OF THE DRAGON SLAYER

Facing the Dragon: Jonathan, David, and a Band of Mighty Men

Yes, relationships with men, like all relationships, come with risk. But it is a risk we must take and learn to manage. The Bible is full of examples that run the gamut of men who passed and failed the tests of brotherhood so we can learn how and how not to cultivate these relationships. When it comes to men who demonstrated remarkable sacrificial, covenant love in friendship, however, the best biblical example (besides Jesus) has to be Jonathan, the son of Saul.

Jonathan met David after his showdown with Goliath. It says that after hearing David tell his father, Saul, of how he fearlessly conquered this giant enemy of Israel, "the soul of Jonathan was knit to the soul of David, and Jonathan loved him as his own soul" (1 Samuel 18:1 ESV). Just a few chapters earlier, the Bible records Jonathan's own brave exploit of taking an entire Philistine garrison with only his armor bearer at his side. Unlike his father Saul, Jonathan had courage born of confidence in the Lord, and the moment he heard that David shared this trait, he recognized him as a brother and loved him. As a result, "Jonathan made a covenant with David, because he loved him as his own soul" (1 Samuel 18:3 ESV).

At first, everything looked promising for these two kindred-spirited warriors. Saul brought David into his household, promoted him as a captain of his army, and gave him his daughter in marriage, making David and Jonathan brothers-in-law. Unsurprisingly, Israel's troops were thrilled to fight under David—who wouldn't be inspired to go into battle with the man who had slain a giant? The problem was that Saul was an aggressive dragon rider absolutely ruled by the fear of competition, and it didn't take long for him to see David's skill, success, and fame as a threat that needed to be crushed. After failing to skewer David with a spear, Saul began trying to convince the men of his court, including Jonathan, to take him out. Jonathan urged his father to reconsider this plan, arguing that David hadn't done him any wrong. But after briefly backing off from his murderous intentions, Saul began throwing spears at David again.

At this point, the writing was on the wall. Saul was going to kill David and anyone who stood in his way. David and Jonathan had an intense conversation in which they came to terms with the reality that David was now a fugitive who needed to flee the country, and Jonathan's life was in danger if he in any way tried to shield David from his father. In response to this dire situation, Jonathan renewed his covenant with David:

> "If I make it through this alive, continue to be my covenant friend. And if I die, keep the covenant friendship with my family—forever. And when God finally rids the earth of David's enemies, stay loyal to Jonathan!" Jonathan repeated his pledge of love and friendship for David. He loved David more than his own soul! (1 Samuel 20:14-17 MSG)

Jonathan was not disloyal to his father, but he knew God was on David's side, and that by making David his enemy, Saul was opposing the Lord. Was Jonathan already aware of the prophet Samuel's pronouncement that God was going to take the kingdom from Saul and give it to a man after His heart? Did he already suspect that David might be the man who would ascend the throne instead of him? We don't know, but his words suggest that he foresaw a time in which David would hold a position of victory over his enemies, including Saul and Saul's house. Yet instead of seeing David as a rival, Jonathan simply asked that David would remain loyal to him. His heart was completely free of any competitive need to protect his position as heir to the kingship from David. He was truly willing to sacrifice everything, even his life, for his covenant friend.

After confirming his father's intention to kill David, Jonathan met with David once more to warn him to flee the country. Weeping, the two men said a final farewell and parted ways, remaining loyal to the end, even though they never saw each other again in life. Years later, when he learned of

Jonathan's death, David lamented, "How the mighty have fallen in the midst of the battle! Jonathan lies slain on your high places. I am distressed for you, my brother Jonathan; very pleasant have you been to me; your love to me was extraordinary, surpassing the love of women" (2 Samuel 1:25-26 ESV).

David's covenant friendship with Jonathan became the high watermark of honor in David's life, and a standard he held to consistently (until his tragic affair with Bathsheba and murder of her husband, Uriah). It was this standard that kept him from killing Saul, despite multiple opportunities and plenty of justifiable reasons for doing so. It was also this standard that caused him to attract a band of fellow renegades—"everyone who was in distress, and everyone who was in debt, and everyone who was bitter in soul" (1 Samuel 22:2)—who eventually all became "mighty men" of war and giant killers under his leadership. Again and again, in battles and other life-threatening situations, David demonstrated that he was a leader who would lay his life down for his men, thus winning their undying devotion and inspiring them to feats of courage.

Scripture is clear that the honor, courage, and integrity that set David and Jonathan apart from weak, insecure men like Saul came from their relationship with the Lord, which was the foundation for their identity. In one critical scene, for example, we see David's men planning to stone him after returning to find their city burned and families and possessions taken by a band of marauding Amakelites. Instead of being blindsided by this show of disloyalty, David "strengthened himself in the LORD his God," and with great effort succeeded in recovering all that had been stolen. This phrase "strengthened himself in the LORD" suggests that whatever David did in that moment helped him to remember who God was to him, who he was, and what he knew to be true based on their history together. He refused to let tragic circumstances or talk of mutiny deflect him from being a man of honor and courage who answered to God before his own friends and brothers. Jonathan displayed the same integrity when he resisted his father's pressure to treat David as a threat instead of a friend.

Once again, we see how the dragons are related. Saul, like Cain, took his insecurities out on other men, but these insecurities were rooted in the breakdown of his relationship with God and with himself. He never really believed what God said about him, and so in a moment of pressure, when the people were scattering from him in fear, he violated God's instructions in an effort to regain control, and forfeited the kingdom (see 1 Samuel 13:8-14). When we drill down into our insecurity with other men, it often sounds like the fear of being controlled or being out of control. Behind that is a misbelief, which is that we can't control ourselves. When God confronted Cain, He essentially said, "Cain, you're the one with the power in this situation. You have the power to do what is right. You have the power to master sin and be a man of honor and virtue. So, what are you going to do?" (see Genesis 4:7 ESV). But Cain refused to strengthen *himself* and access the power of self-control God was making available to him. Both he and Saul discovered that when they tried to control or eliminate other men instead of trying to control themselves, they only ended up more controlled by the fear of man. As Proverbs 29:25 says, "Fear of man will prove to be a snare, but whoever trusts in the LORD is kept safe" (NIV).

David and Jonathan, on the other hand, knew God and knew who they were in Him, which freed them from the fear of man and led them to focus on controlling themselves and honoring God, no matter what anyone around them was doing. Self-control, grounded in a secure relationship with the Father and the secure identity we receive from Him, is what unlocks responsibility and honor in our relationships with men. Being able to tell ourselves what to do according to our core values and God-given calling—and actually do it—is what turns competition from a zero-sum game into the iron-sharpening exercise it was intended to be, and turns sacrifice and covenant friendships into the most meaningful and enriching things in our lives.

THE WAY OF THE DRAGON SLAYER

The Way of the Dragon Slayer: Building Covenant Friendships

Dave Ramsey uses an illustration to describe the power of unity in marriage that applies just as well to brotherhood.[16] He explained that a single Belgian draft horse can pull 8,000 pounds, leading most of us to imagine that two horses pulling together could pull twice as much, 16,000 pounds. In fact, two horses can pull 24,000 pounds—three times what one can pull alone. What is more, when those two horses are trained for six weeks to pull together, the weight they can manage rises to 32,000 pounds. This calls to mind the promise of Leviticus 26:8: "Five of you shall chase a hundred, and a hundred of you shall put ten thousand to flight." When men band together and work to accomplish something, the strength and effectiveness of each multiplies, creating exponential benefit for those they are protecting, providing for, and connecting.

The question is, how do we get men to pull together? How can they see and experience the power of healthy competition, accountability, and sacrificial love that will sharpen them into "mighty men"? The answer is that we must *become* covenant-hearted men, and *find* other covenant-hearted men.

Since ancient times, covenants have typically been made with some kind of ritual involving blood-letting or sacrifice, symbolizing what is being promised and owed to the other person in the relationship. The heart of covenant says, "I will sacrifice my own comfort, resources, and life to benefit you." To this day, men who go to war together consistently forge deep friendships, because on the battlefield their success and survival depend on each other—their mission calls forth covenant love and sacrifice. But without the same awareness of a great purpose with life-and-death stakes, most men struggle to recognize that they need each other just as much on the battlefields of civilian life—at work, at home, at church, in the community, and when they're alone—and to make the sacrifices that will truly benefit them. Yet it is on these battlefields that the true war—the spiritual, cosmic war between the

---

16 | Dave Ramsey, "The Power of Unity," YouTube video, https://www.youtube.com/watch?v=KRTeLGSNPug.

forces of Jesus and the dragon—is being played out every day in our lives. If we truly wish to become covenant-hearted men, then we must cultivate a mindset that we will not survive this war without brothers-in-arms who will fight for and with us.

One of the most direct ways to test and reveal a covenant heart is to look at how we pursue and respond to feedback. By now it should be clear that feedback is one of our greatest needs in all our important relationships—with God, ourselves, our wives, and our friendships. A man who is committed to protecting "me" before "us" will not seek or listen to feedback, but a true dragon slayer has an unquenchable hunger and curiosity to learn how these people are experiencing him and how he needs to adjust to help the relationship thrive. The quest for feedback is an essential expression of humility, which "comes before honor" (Proverbs 15:33). I define honor in a relationship as "two powerful people working together to meet the needs of each other and the situation." Of course, feedback in each of these relationships is going to sound and look different. The way God talks to you is different from the way you talk to yourself or the way your wife talks to you. When it comes to our brothers, feedback often looks like what the Bible calls "the slap of a friend," or as I like to call it, "the brotherly shove." Brotherly love isn't passive—it will shove you when you need to adjust and get back in line with your identity and calling. It is also not above using healthy shame, which is pain specifically inflicted to help you realize that what you are doing is harmful to yourself and others and beneath who you were created and called to be. One night at dinner I saw a friend throw back four drinks at dinner and render himself incapable of driving home. Afterwards I gave him a shove: "What the heck, man? What were you thinking? You do know that doing stuff like this is a good way to blow up your whole world, right?" He received it for what it was and agreed, "You're right."

If you haven't had a brotherly shove recently, then there's a good chance that you're hiding in your relationships with men and isolating yourself. Craig once told me that one of the first signs a guy he's mentoring is about to do something stupid that could blow up his life is that he starts to skip meetings for coffee or other events where other men could see what he's doing. "Isolation doesn't allow for small corrections," he said. "Small corrections prevent big mistakes." I've seen the same problem at work in the lives of toxic or fallen leaders. Many of these men have learned to hide in plain sight. They have teams and oversight boards and other systems that are supposed to be keeping them accountable, but these turn out to be a facade because none of these people have permission to give these men a brotherly shove when they need it. One leader I spoke to in recent years told me that in three decades of ministry, no one had ever talked to him the way I talked to him about the weaknesses that were threatening to compromise him. "We all need someone who will talk to us like this," I said, "Especially someone in your position."

In his book *Men on Fire*, Stephen Mansfield says we need to create a "Free Fire Zone" with our chosen band of brothers:

> I use the phrase Free Fire Zone to describe a condition among a band of men in which anything that needs to be said to make any one of them better will be said. It is a state in which a group of men have agreed that they are committed to each other's good and that they will address anything that needs to be addressed in a man's life to help him be his best.
>
> Not only will these men speak to the issues in a man's life but they will then join him in his fight. They will coach him if they can. They will get him coaching if they can't. They will pray for him, hold him accountable, and cheer him on until victory is achieved.[17]

---

17 | Stephen Mansfield, *Men on Fire*, (Grand Rapids, MI: Baker Publishing Group, 2020) Kindle Edition, 97.

Creating and maintaining a Free Fire Zone is a process. Mansfield describes two stages that will help us create a safe place for this level of honesty and accountability with other men. First, there's Indirect Connection. This is the stage where you're getting to know each other by doing things together. You can learn a lot about a man by watching how he acts and interacts during a Super Bowl party, Crossfit workout, hunting trip, or concert. Eventually you'll be able to discern if he is someone with an "edge" of strength, character, and skills who can bring a sharpening influence into your life. From there, you can progress to the Calling in Reinforcements stage. "This is when you ask a man you already know to help you with something he's better at doing than you are," Mansfield explains, adding, "You want to be careful here. We are not trying to manipulate. We are also not trying to bring the man into the core of our lives too suddenly. Instead, you want to move the friendship, naturally and casually, toward being helpful as well as fun."[18] Once you have established that this is a relationship in which you both have the desire and ability to help each other grow and improve, you can begin to step towards increasing levels of trust and openness in your communication with one another.

Mastering the art of trust-building is critical if we hope to find other covenant-hearted men. Sadly, "covenant" has become a trigger word for many who have experienced their trust being exploited instead of protected. Over the years in ministry I have met many men who left large churches and other organizations after years of service because they were essentially betrayed by leaders who invited them into covenant but didn't honor it. These leaders made big promises about how they would build and partner together, but this turned out to be a bait and switch to the actual, one-sided deal, which was that the leader would be faithful as long as these men were sacrificing to serve his vision. As a result, these men ended up devoting years serving in roles that they hoped would lead to greater responsibility, influence, and effectiveness with their own gifts, but the moment they tried

---

18 | Mansfield, *Men on Fire*, 101.

to step out of the sandbox the leader had put them in, they were blocked or punished. While it's impossible to manage all risk in relationships, and betrayal will probably happen to all of us at some point, we can often save ourselves from pouring into a relationship that's not going to produce the fruit we want by making sure it passes through trust-building stages and reaches a Free Fire Zone before we sell the farm and commit to going the distance in a covenant partnership.

We won't build trust successfully if we don't have boundaries when trust is not being honored. For example, when a younger man reaches out to Craig for mentoring, he will extend a certain measure of access to the guy—he will let him have his phone number, be responsive to texts and calls, and schedule regular meetups for coffee. If the guy starts showing up late or missing their meetings, Craig will address it and extend a number of chances for him to adjust. He has a lot of grace for guys with backgrounds of abuse and bullying who are still getting used to the idea of opening up to another man, and he wants them to feel safe with him. He shows them that he is willing to sacrifice his time and effort for the relationship. But if after multiple chances they don't reciprocate and show that they have some skin in the game, he lets them know that he's not going to be calling or texting to check in with them or scheduling any more meetups.

The good news is that if you have a covenant heart, it is possible to find fathers and brothers like Craig out there who are truly willing to lay down their lives for their spiritual sons and friends. One of these fathers in my own life was a man named John Tillery. John took me under his wing at the beginning of my first career in social work. He sponsored my university education to complete a master's degree, and made it clear that he was grooming me to replace him in our organization. When the Lord interrupted my plans and called me into pastoral ministry, I was nervous to talk to John and let him know that I was not going to be able to fulfill that dream. But when I explained the situation to him, he didn't miss a beat. He said, "If I have done anything to invest in what God was doing in your future, I count it as an honor." He truly cared about me and his reward in our relationship was seeing me rise to become the best man, husband, father, social worker, and leader I could be. As I see it, everything I have accomplished is credited to John's account, along with the other fathers and brothers who have invested in me. I'm now endeavoring to honor their example in the lives of my children, Loving on Purpose team, and close friendships. If I can pass the baton of covenant to men who will carry that standard in their own lives, I will have succeeded.

ACTIVATE THE WAY OF THE DRAGON SLAYER

DEFINE THE DRAGON

The enemy first separated man from his Father, and then brother from his brother by deceiving one into taking his insecurities out on the other. The story of Cain and Abel points to the immense stakes surrounding relationships between men. When men live united in covenant together, we maximize the elements of masculinity for the benefit of all those around us. The call of God on our lives is to push through the insecurities, competition, and failings in each of us and form the catalytic bond of brotherly love. The gates of hell shall not prevail against a society of unified, godly men.

POINTS OF ATTACK

- Competition: I end up creating a win/lose dynamic with this man. Whenever I am with him, I am trying to never be the "loser." I ruin the bond by making him a threat rather than a brother.
- Covenant: Make a commitment to someone for life? Lay my life down for my brother? What's in this for me? This stirs my own feelings of being an inadequate friend/man.

- Sacrifice: Will I cultivate the love and courage to invest in the lives of other men who are frail in character and will fall short at times? Am I committed to the discomfort of maturing in my love?
- Isolation: Selfishness and foolishness await me in the den of my disconnected life. Arrogance and delusion will guide me in my isolation.

LESSONS LEARNED

- I was created to run with my brothers for life.
- Life is easier when I pull together with other men who are on the same journey to glorify God.
- I multiply the strength of my lives in partnership with my brothers.
- I surround myself with brothers who will give me a "brotherly shove" when I need one.
- I will courageously speak the truth in love to my brothers as needed.
- I will make and keep the goal of connection with my brothers for the rest of my life!

THE SWORD

> A man who has friends must himself be friendly,
>
> But there is a friend who sticks closer than a brother. (Proverbs 18:24)

> Now when he had finished speaking to Saul, the soul of Jonathan was knit to the soul of David, and Jonathan loved him as his own soul. Saul took him that day, and would not let him go home to his father's house anymore. Then Jonathan and

David made a covenant, because he loved him as his own soul. And Jonathan took off the robe that was on him and gave it to David, with his armor, even to his sword and his bow and his belt. (1 Samuel 18:1-4)

This is My commandment, that you love one another as I have loved you. Greater love has no one than this, than to lay down one's life for his friends. No longer do I call you servants, for a servant does not know what his master is doing; but I have called you friends, for all things that I heard from My Father I have made known to you. You did not choose Me, but I chose you and appointed you that you should go and bear fruit, and that your fruit should remain, that whatever you ask the Father in My name He may give you. (John 15:12-15)

Let love be without hypocrisy. Abhor what is evil. Cling to what is good. Be kindly affectionate to one another with brotherly love, in honor giving preference to one another; not lagging in diligence, fervent in spirit, serving the Lord; rejoicing in hope, patient in tribulation, continuing steadfastly in prayer; distributing to the needs of the saints, given to hospitality. (Romans 12: 9-13)

HOW TO SLAY

1. Reflect.

    a. Does the sign over my head read "Feedback Welcome" or does it say "Don't You Dare!"?

    b. Who am I getting to know and being drawn to through Indirect Connection activities? What strengths do I see in them that I need in my life?

    c. Who am I calling on for reinforcements in my life? Who is calling on me? Am I building trust through the exchange of help with other men? ?

    d. Who have I built a Free Fire Zone with? Are we fulfilling our covenant duty to call each other higher? Am I speaking up when I see something that needs to change? Are these men doing the same for me?

2. Connect.

    a. Discuss the conclusions of your reflection exercise with the other men in your group.

3. Adjust.

    a. Participate in Indirect Connection. Get a group of guys together to do something fun.

    b. Reach out to a friend you want to "sharpen" you in a particular area.

    c. Invite a trusted friend to step into the Free Fire Zone and give you feedback on where you can grow and improve in your life.

CHAPTER 6
MAN WITH NATURE

There are many stories I could tell about my friend Wesley Kotys' adventures in the great outdoors—adventures that have brought him face to face with dangers that would make any man aware of his own mortality. (Our trip to Kodiak Island was just one of his many hunting expeditions!) But to his own surprise, his greatest battle with "nature" ended up taking place in a hospital.

Wes and his wife Sarah are two of the godliest people I know. After meeting at a church retreat and both hearing from the Lord that they would marry each other, they got to know each other during a three-year courtship and then became husband and wife. A couple of years later, they felt ready to start their family. Yet when months passed, then a year, and then another year with Sarah not getting pregnant, they started to wonder if something was wrong. Their doctors assured them they were healthy—there was no obvious reason why they were experiencing infertility. They continued to pray and hope, but years of disappointment kept stacking up, causing grief that tested them spiritually and emotionally at a level they had never experienced. Sarah in particular was tormented by the idea that the problem had to lie with her, despite there being no sign that this was the case. Wes struggled to comfort and reassure her while wrestling with his own questions and sadness about why things weren't working the way they had hoped and expected.

Finally, after eight years of failure to conceive naturally, they decided to pursue in vitro fertilization. The miraculous day came when they took a pregnancy test and it was positive. As this new life grew in Sarah's womb, the hopes and dreams they had all but buried began to return. The pregnancy progressed normally, mom and baby were both healthy, and everything looked great . . . until it was time to deliver their little boy.

Sarah wanted the delivery to be as natural as possible, but when she failed to go into labor on her own, the doctors decided to induce her. Finally, after three sleepless days and nights at the hospital, baby Dominic made his appearance. The doctors were surprised to find him blue and with the umbilical cord wrapped twice around his neck, as the ultrasound and other fetal monitors had not given them any sign that he was in distress, and immediately went to work to get him breathing. Thankfully, he soon turned pink and began to cry. Wes and Sarah shared a brief, blissful moment together gazing at their beautiful newborn son. Only moments later, just after the doctors finished removing the placenta, Sarah started to hemorrhage blood and blacked out. A nurse handed Dominic to Wes, who stood by helplessly as the medical team, which had grown to nearly twenty people by now, rushed to stop his wife from bleeding out. By the time they succeeded, Sarah had lost nearly sixty percent of the blood in her body and was hanging by a thread, in need of an immediate transfusion to save her life.

Shellshocked, exhausted, and alone, Wes was forced to hold vigil in the hospital waiting room while the medical team took his unconscious wife to the ICU. For twenty-four hours, between brief visits with his newborn son in the nursery, he paced the halls, praying and wrestling with the possibility that after nearly a decade of praying and contending for this miracle child, he might be forced to raise him as a single father. Pain, fear, frustration, and anger rolled through him in waves as he continued to grapple with his feeling of powerlessness. No gun or any other weapon he possessed could help him neutralize this threat to the person he had vowed to love and protect with his life. But he wasn't about to let her go. His anguish became so intense at one point that, without caring who heard him, he shouted aloud to the Lord in the waiting room, "I'm not trading my wife for my son! That was not the deal! I need You to bring her through this."

Finally, the doctors came with a good report. Sarah was conscious and recovering. Wes was allowed to visit her and they soon brought baby Dominic to her as well. A few days later, mom and baby were both released from the hospital. The shadow of death had passed over their family.

In the weeks and months following Dominic's birth, Wes found himself experiencing anxiety, moments of panic, insomnia, and other signs of post-traumatic stress. He had never dealt with symptoms like this, even though he had been in a number of dangerous and life-threatening situations. Sarah had no such symptoms, as she had no memory of anything that had happened from the moment she passed out in the delivery room. Only Wes had been fully conscious on the battleground of birth, pain, life, and death where the fate of their family hung in the balance. He had never been more terrified in his entire life than he was during those twenty-four hours.

Wes's anxiety failed to resolve naturally as he progressed in his journey as a new father, and he found himself living in a state of tension. On one hand, he was delighting in watching Dominic grow and develop, while on the other, a new hyper-protective instinct inside him was constantly being triggered. He found himself saying "Be careful!" around Dominic a lot, which was new for him. He had always been a risk-taker in life, whether in business, outdoor adventuring, or his faith. This new obsession with keeping his son away from all risk was so out of character for Wes that Sarah confronted him on a few occasions and asked why he wasn't being himself.

Wes stayed in "careful" mode until the inevitable happened—Dominic got hurt. At two years old, he fell down a couple of steps and suffered an unusual spiral fracture in one of his legs. As Wes watched his son recovering with his leg in a cast, reality confronted him. There was no way he could protect Dominic from all harm in life. The fact that he had been trying so hard to do so revealed that he was not thinking rationally. In fact, he was convicted that he had been trying to play God in his son's life, and it was turning him into an anxious control freak. This was a problem and he needed to deal with it.

Wes began to face his fear in his own prayer time with the Lord, and also sought prayer and inner healing ministry. During one of these ministry sessions, the prayer counselor asked Wes if he knew "where Jesus was" during the traumatic events at the hospital. Wes realized this was part of why the experience had been so terrifying—instead of feeling the presence of the Holy Spirit as he usually was able to, he hadn't been able to sense Him at all throughout the whole ordeal. Instead, he had felt alone, extremely sleep-deprived, and completely exhausted—one of the most emotionally vulnerable states any person can be in—as well as helpless and powerless.

When he asked the Lord to show him where He had been, he started to notice certain details he hadn't fully appreciated before. He remembered Sarah's OB/GYN telling him that what happened to Sarah was like "déjà vu" because she had just been through the same situation with another woman who had started bleeding out in the delivery room. Thanks to that experience, she knew exactly what to do, stayed calm under pressure, and wasted no time in treating Sarah and saving her life. Meanwhile, because Sarah had "coded" and been sent to the ICU, the CEO of the hospital, a good friend of Wes's, heard about it and sent a message for the hospital staff to give Sarah the highest level of care and support they could provide. Then there was a nurse, a friend of Sarah's, who helped hold Dominic and encourage Wes as he waited to hear about Sarah's condition. God hadn't prevented the crisis, but He had put the people in place who would bring their family safely through it.

Reassured that God truly was in control and protecting his wife and son, Wes was able to release the fear he had carried for two years to the Lord and start walking in peace again. He also shifted his goal from trying to be "careful" with Dominic, which would only teach him to fear risk, to the goal of raising his son with a love of adventure and the skill and mental toughness to manage pain and difficulty. In the years since making this shift, Wes has introduced Dominic to all kinds of dangerous and thrilling experiences, from riding motorcycles to hunting. He loves seeing his son take risks, pick himself up when he gets hurt, and look to him for courage and guidance in the process. Through it all, he is teaching Dominic that the best way to live his life is to the full, without fear.

THE WAY OF THE DRAGON SLAYER

The Nature of the Dragon:
The Fear of Insignificance, Vulnerability, and Eternity

It might seem a bit odd to start a chapter on man's relationship with the natural world with a story about infertility and difficult childbirth. Don't worry—I have more "nature" stories to tell in this chapter, including one about how my friend Joe Huston earned the nickname "Bear Snack." (Yes, another bear story!) But when we look at the origin of man's relationship with nature and how it was designed, we find that the dragon we must slay in this relationship is the very one Wes encountered in that hospital—the fear of insignificance, vulnerability, and eternity.

The creation account in Genesis shows God hovering over a dark, empty, chaotic wasteland and bringing into it light, life, and order. His work crescendos with the final act of creating a man to be His partner as a cultivator and caretaker of this newmade world. In fact, reading between the lines in Genesis 2, we find that man's role as a protector, provider, and connector was first directed at the natural world before God created Eve and enabled Adam to start a family. His first assignment was to tend and guard the garden—the initial outpost of God-man civilization on the as-yet untamed earth—and to name the animals. The origin of the word "husband" reflects this:

> Late Old English (in the senses 'male head of a household' and 'manager, steward'), from Old Norse *húsbóndi* 'master of a house', from *hús* 'house' + *bóndi* 'occupier and tiller of the soil'. The original sense of the verb was 'till, cultivate'.[19]

"Husbandry" retains this original meaning of the caretaking and cultivation of land, animals, and natural resources. Adam was trained in the school of husbanding creation before becoming a husband to his wife—not because she was second in importance, but because this training gave him essential

---

19 | s.v., "husband," *Oxford American Dictionary.*

preparation for him to fulfill his role in both relationships. This training didn't involve dirt, sweat, and back-breaking labor either—those only came in after he fell. It was training through discovery, adventure, and romance.

In *Fathered by God*, John Eldredge describes how a boy first journeys through the Cowboy and Warrior stages, in which his heart awakens to the call to venture out into the wild world and confront the dangers he encounters there. But then he hears a different call—the call to Beauty. Beauty awakens his heart to love, and it is the Lover who ultimately embraces the role of husband, both to the natural world and to his wife. Eve is "the personification of Beauty," John explains, but the man's first awakening to Beauty "often . . . comes in the world of Nature".[20] This awakening leads him on a quest for a new kind of knowledge that goes beyond facts, analysis, and reason—knowledge that is aesthetic, relational, and ultimately spiritual. For if he follows this quest to the end, he finds that what he was seeking in the beauty of nature and the beauty of the woman was not those things but the source of beauty Himself. The beauty of creation—the natural world and the woman—is a great love poem displaying the beauty of the Creator, and the "aha" for the man is realizing that He is the One who has been wooing and romancing him all along.

God's intention for Adam in the garden was not to train him as an employee, but as a son who shared His love for everything He created, and through that love to become His partner in causing the natural world to flourish. He thus led Adam on a journey of introducing Himself as Adam's Provider, Protector, and Connector, for only by receiving and learning from the source would he become who he was created to be. The choice to eat the fruit of the tree of the knowledge of good and evil was the choice to go outside of that relationship to seek the knowledge of beauty—to elevate the created above the Creator. Thus Adam not only broke his relationships with God and Eve, but also with the natural world he was created to love and steward. And so came the devastating consequence: "therefore the LORD

---

20 | John Eldredge, *Fathered by God*, (Nashville, TN: Thomas Nelson, 2009), 128.

God sent him out from the garden of Eden to work the ground from which he was taken. He drove out the man, and at the east of the garden of Eden he placed the cherubim and a flaming sword that turned every way to guard the way to the tree of life" (Genesis 3:23-24 ESV).

The word "drove out" also means "divorce." God had to divorce the man from the place of beauty and eternal life and exile him to the wilderness. This was a protection—apparently it is much worse to live forever in a fallen state than it is to die. But it also permanently established the change in man's relationship with nature. Estrangement from the Creator meant that creation would no longer recognize man in the same way as its caretaker. Though its beauty would still call to his heart, it would also remind him of his spiritual alienation. Though its animals and plants would still nourish him, they would also be under a curse, producing "thorns and thistles" (Genesis 3:18) and being, as Tennyson put it, "red in tooth and claw." Instead of being the home where he would rule and reign with his Father forever, the natural world became the place where he must struggle to survive, and the place where he would surely die.

Over millennia, men have carved out outposts of "civilization," to the point where today, entire generations can grow up without ever really being exposed to the vast remaining stretches of wilderness across the globe. The hospital is one place where the reality of nature continues to intrude in the place where man likes to believe he has conquered it. But if a modern man does go out to wild country, he will confront two uncomfortable realities. First, the immensity of wide open spaces, the height of mountain peaks, the roar of white water, the bowl of stars shining down on him unfiltered by city lights, and the unfamiliar movements of weather in the sky and creatures in the woods will remind him that he is small, insignificant, vulnerable, and easy to kill. His brains, money, and whatever gear he brought to survive the elements can quickly seem useless when a storm rolls in or a predator attacks. Nature doesn't ask his permission. In fact, nature doesn't really seem to acknowledge his existence. Rain, cold, heat, lightning, wild animals, falling trees, rising waters, crushing winds, and snow were all going to happen with or without him there. He just showed up and put himself in danger, and danger is now with him.

The second uncomfortable reality that will press on his awareness is the question of what governs creation. To the untrained observer, weather patterns and the ways of flora and fauna can seem random, or at most, merely governed by primal forces and instincts. But anyone willing to pay attention to the natural world will quickly notice that it is exceedingly orderly and complex. Only those who cling to ignorance can hold the idea that nature is governed by meaningless laws and a mindless process of evolution. There is a Creator who made all of this . . . and made him. And where does he stand with that Creator? His eternal fate hangs on the answer.

THE WAY OF THE DRAGON SLAYER

Riding the Dragon: Hard Hearts

This secular city dweller is the type we might imagine when we think of a man who has a dysfunctional relationship with nature. But preferring an urban environment to the wilderness doesn't necessarily make you a dragon rider, or even unmanly. There is a place in the world for what Brant Hansen terms the "avid indoorsman." Modern civilization could not exist without a division of labor in which some men work in farms, fields, forests, rivers, and oceans, while others take up their posts in classrooms, boardrooms, factory floors, and storefronts. What leads men to become dragon riders in their relationship with the natural world lies not in the place where man lives and works, but in his heart. Standing Bear said, "Man's heart away from nature becomes hard." While I certainly recommend that every man leaves the indoors for the outdoors on a regular basis, you don't necessarily have to pull a Henry David Thoreau and go live in the woods to keep your heart from becoming hard. What keeps a man's heart in the right place—or leads it astray—always has to do with what he *worships*.

In Romans 1, Paul diagnoses the classic breakdown that happens to humans and our relationships with ourselves and the created world when our worship strays from God:

> For since the creation of the world God's invisible qualities—his eternal power and divine nature—have been clearly seen, being understood from what has been made, so that people are without excuse. For although they knew God, they neither glorified him as God nor gave thanks to him, but their thinking became futile and their foolish hearts were darkened. Although they claimed to be wise, they became fools and exchanged the glory of the immortal God for images made to look like a mortal human being and birds and animals and

reptiles . . . They exchanged the truth about God for a lie, and worshiped and served created things rather than the Creator—who is forever praised. Amen. (Romans 1:20-23, 25 NIV)

"Although they claimed to be wise, they became fools." This certainly describes our culture today. We live in the information age, built on the foundation of science and industry. Our scientific knowledge and innovation has given us power over nature like never before. We can extract every type of mineral resource from the ground. We can harness electricity from oil, gas, wind, sun, and water. We can modify crops and even the weather. We can build machines that allow us to penetrate from deep space to the depths of the ocean. We can develop medicines to conquer the most deadly viruses, bacteria, and cancers. We can even change our own DNA. Yet just because we *can* do something doesn't tell us that we *should* do it, or *how* we should do it. Only wisdom can tell us those things. Wisdom flows from the knowledge behind scientific knowledge—the knowledge of God and how He designed humans and creation to flourish together. Whenever we refuse to worship the God who made the world, we become fractured in our understanding of how we ought to view, use, and care for it. Here are just a few dragon riders wandering the planet today who have rejected God's wisdom in their relationship with nature:

The power-driven industrialist. These are the obvious aggressive dragon riders of the natural world, the latest incarnation of the emperors and kings of old who see the beauty and riches of nature as a source of wealth to be accumulated and exploited at scale—not just because they are insatiably greedy for more, but because they seek power to become significant, invulnerable, and ultimately, immortal. They pervert their businesses, organizations, and governments into a corporate matrix that bribes masses of people into supporting and executing their wealth-making projects, many of which start out, at least on the surface, with a noble-enough humanitarian mission, but which so often end up harming the environment and their workers.

The mindless consumer. This passive dragon rider is the ideal citizen and worker in the industrialists' utopia. He is the toxic avid indoorsman—the one who thinks everything, from the food he eats to the clothes he wears to the devices he uses, comes from the store. He has never tried to cultivate any real knowledge, appreciation, or love for the natural world. For him, nature is not a place of beauty and awe, but of unnecessary discomfort and danger. He doesn't really care to know more about either the benefits or harms created by human development of nature or take responsibility for his part in them—he just wants to continue using them to make his life as comfortable, pleasurable, and easy as possible.

The extreme environmentalist. This man is the reactionary to the excesses of the industrialists and the consumers. He goes beyond the traditional environmentalist, who seeks to mitigate the harms while retaining the benefits of man's development of the natural world, and seems to think that the best relationship man can have with nature is to leave it completely alone. Men in this category are typically young revolutionary types hungry for meaning and purpose. At schools and universities, they have been indoctrinated to deconstruct traditional worldviews while embracing a number of myths—the most alarming of which include that a catastrophic manmade climate crisis is imminent; that the world will shortly be overpopulated, creating catastrophic food shortages; that human beings are "parasites" who have only impacted the natural world for the worse as exploiters; and that it would be better to forego having children and for the number of people on the planet to be drastically reduced.

These may sound like caricatures, but you don't have to look hard to find people in each of these categories. They tend to expose themselves through acts of hypocrisy, corruption, and insistence on solutions that end up being just as or more problematic than the issues they are claiming to solve. They moralize about "lowering emissions" while traveling by private jets and maintaining lifestyles that consume vastly more energy and resources than the average person. They embrace and preach vegetarianism and veganism simply because they don't want animals to be harmed, without understanding the actual process, costs, and impacts of farming or food production on the environment or our health. They are also generally from wealthy, developed countries and much of their vision for global "sustainability" sounds tone deaf to the rest of the world because it generally doesn't involve helping poorer nations achieve the same level of wealth and development.

Michael Shellenberger, who describes himself as a "humanitarian environmentalist," exposes the problems with all of these dragon riders in his book *Apocalypse Never: Why Environmental Alarmism Hurts Us All*. In each chapter of the book, he lays out the facts of most of the pressing environmental issues facing the world today, as well as the best solutions currently available. The problem, he argues, is that the industrialists, consumers, and extreme environmentalists are all resistant to these solutions, because they are all opposed, for different reasons, to pursuing the goal—which is, in fact, a biblical goal—of mutual flourishing for humanity and nature.

Shellenberger is particularly insightful in pointing out that people are embracing extreme environmentalism today out of a religious impulse. Yet again, they are replacing the worship of the Creator with the worship of creation, and it is only producing anxiety and a lack of wisdom about our role and responsibility as cultivators and caretakers:

> Environmentalism today is the dominant secular religion of the educated, upper-middle-class elite in most developed and many developing nations. It provides a new story about our collective and individual purpose. It designates good guys and bad guys, heroes and villains. And it does so in the language of science, which provides it with legitimacy.
>
> On the one hand, environmentalism and its sister religion, vegetarianism, appear to be a radical break

from the Judeo-Christian religious tradition. For starters, environmentalists themselves do not tend to be believers, or strong believers, in Judeo-Christianity. In particular, environmentalists reject the view that humans have, or should have, dominion, or control, over Earth.

On the other hand, apocalyptic environmentalism is a kind of new Judeo-Christian religion, one that has replaced God with nature. In the Judeo-Christian tradition, human problems stem from our failure to adjust ourselves to God. In the apocalyptic environmental tradition, human problems stem from our failure to adjust ourselves to nature . . .

The trouble with the new environmental religion is that it has become increasingly apocalyptic, destructive, and self-defeating. It leads its adherents to demonize their opponents, often hypocritically. It drives them to seek to restrict power and prosperity at home and abroad. And it spreads anxiety and depression without meeting the deeper psychological, existential, and spiritual needs its ostensibly secular devotees seek.[21]

Rejecting Christianity does not free people from their need to worship something that gives them a purpose around which to order their lives. Shellenberger notes that this deep spiritual need is driven by what Ernest Becker called "the denial of death." The fear of death drives humans to seek

---

21 | Michael Shellenberger, *Apocalypse Never,* (New York, NY: HarperCollins, 2020), 263-265.

an "immortality project" that gives our lives a sense of meaning that transcends death. But the only immortality offered by the new environmental religion seems to be a perverse living martyrdom that is robbing young people of mental and physical health, a family legacy, and the opportunity for them to enjoy and care for the natural world without fear and guilt. This new religion in the name of nature actually leads us to the same place as the exploiters and consumers—away from nature and to a hard heart.

THE WAY OF THE DRAGON SLAYER

Facing the Dragon: But Did You Die?

I promised I would tell you Joe Huston's bear story. Joe is a long-time friend, fellow hunter, former military, and Alaskan bush pilot who can make a plane do things you just didn't know they could do. He is just shy of an air acrobat for a living, and will certainly get you to pucker up with some of the antics he does during a casual landing along the face of a glacier (I speak from personal experience!).

In 1997, Joe was stationed at the Tikchik Lodge Seaplane Base on a small peninsula between Nuyakuk Lake and Tikchik Lake, deep in the Alaskan bush. On the first of July, he started his day as usual with calisthenics, followed by a jog down the 1,800-foot gravel runway. He had just started jogging back to the base when he heard bushes rustling. Glancing behind him, he saw a brown bear on his tail, only thirty feet back and gaining. He sprinted a few more steps before remembering you can't outrun a bear and shouldn't try, then turned around and began waving his arms at it, yelling, "Go home!" The bear stopped momentarily, then began to circle Joe, cutting him off from the runway back to the lodge.

Joe barely had time to register the certain knowledge that he was in trouble before the bear struck him from behind. A massive paw hit Joe's back, its claws puncturing his right lung, while the other came down on his right thigh, knocking him off his feet and smashing him face-first into the gravel. He managed to raise his head and look back in time to see the bear sinking its teeth into his right thigh. After tearing off a few chunks of muscle, the bear went for Joe's shoulder, lifting him off the ground and shaking him like a rag doll. He could hear his bones crunching in the bear's jaws.

At this point, Joe knew, *This is it. I'm going to die.* A split second later, however, he remembered! He had just read a book with a number of stories of people who survived bear attacks by playing dead. Immediately, he went as limp as he could, closed his eyes, and held his breath. Within moments, the bear stopped shaking him and dropped him on the ground. Joe felt the bear's breath on his face as it inspected him. Then, to his amazement, he heard it shuffling away back into the bushes.

Joe held his breath until he couldn't anymore. As he sucked in air and breathed out again, he heard it blowing out from the wound in his back. Joe knew his condition was critical. His only hope was to try and make it back to the lodge. Through a sheer will to survive and fear that the bear would return, he got to his feet. His legs were torn and bleeding, but not broken. Staggering forward, he managed to traverse the rest of the runway and reach one of the lodge cabins. The staff member who answered the door immediately froze in horror upon seeing Joe's mangled, blood-soaked body.

"Go get the owner," Joe wheezed.

The woman ran off toward the main lodge and four other staff members soon rushed to help a now collapsed Joe. They managed to wrap him in towels to stop the bleeding and then hustle him out to the Cessna 206 that was the lodge's only transportation back to the closest town, Dillingham, Alaska. The lodge owner soon appeared, carrying a "stat" kit of emergency medical supplies and accompanied by a lodge guest who happened to be an anesthesiologist. As the owner fired up the plane, Joe remembered it only had an hour or so of fuel left in it, as he had flown it back from Anchorage the night before. He could only hope it was enough to get them to the hospital in Dillingham.

As the lodge owner took the plane in the air, the anesthesiologist began searching for a vein in Joe's arm to start an IV. By this point he could hardly speak with one lung fully collapsed, the other one on the verge of collapse, severe blood loss, and his entire body rigid with excruciating pain. Panting, he begged her for a shot of morphine.

Unable to find a vein, she put down her needle and looked Joe straight in the eyes. "Are you saved?" she asked. "Do you know Jesus Christ?"

Joe's heart sank. If this lady was giving him last rites, she must be certain he wasn't going to make it. Then he remembered that he had accepted Jesus as a child when his family had briefly attended church.

"Yes," Joe answered.

She began to pray the Lord's prayer. To Joe's surprise, the fear that had gripped him since he first caught sight of that bear lifted off of him. Though he was still in terrible pain, he now felt a deep peace. Whether he lived or died, everything would be okay.

Despite low fuel and dangerous low-lying fog, the lodge owner successfully landed the plane at the Dillingham airport, where an ambulance was waiting to rush Joe to the Kanakanak Hospital. After stabilizing and intubating him, they loaded him on a life flight to Anchorage, where he underwent wound care and multiple surgeries to rebuild his shoulder. After the first surgery, he asked the doctor how close he had come to dying.

"The carotid artery in your neck was exposed in the shoulder wound," the doctor said. "Another fraction of an inch and you would have bled out right there on the runway after that bear mauled you."

Joe could only conclude that God had kept him alive for a purpose, and that He wanted Joe to know Him. From that point on, he dedicated his life to pursuing Jesus. He also went right back to doing what he had been doing, and what he loved—living out in the Alaskan wilderness, flying planes, exercising (though he became much more careful about where he jogged), fishing, and hunting. He has even hunted bears, though not out of revenge. His nickname, "Bear Snack," has created many opportunities for him to tell his story and remind people, and himself, that the One who created us and bears is also Lord over life and death, and we can trust Him.

Not everyone gets a near-death experience like Joe, and not all who do come out of it with faith in Jesus. But those who do agree that the realization "I could have died" can change your life. For many, it's where they get delivered from the fear of death. They return to their lives as Joe did, with an abiding sense of meaning and mission. They know that in a world full of forces both natural and supernatural, God is the force that is keeping them alive for His purposes. And death, when it comes, is not the end, but merely a door they pass through on their way to eternity with Him.

One of the things I love about taking wilderness adventures with my band of brothers is that we often taste enough nature danger to remind us of the truths of our mortality—and of our hope of eternity in Christ. Every time, we return from these trips with crazy stories to tell, and just as importantly, with our hearts recalibrated. We are freshly aligned with and alive to our purpose on the planet, and reinvigorated to pursue it with passion.

Again, while I highly recommend that all men should go outdoors as often as possible, the good news is that we don't need to face off with an Alaskan bear to be set free of the fear of insignificance, vulnerability, and eternity. The thing that sets us free of this fear is the revelation of Jesus' victory over death in our lives, and we can have it anywhere—in a hospital room, at a coffee shop, on a boat, or around a campfire. Hebrews 2:14-15 says, "Since the children have flesh and blood, he too shared in their humanity so that by his death he might break the power of him who holds the power of death—that is, the devil—and free those who all their lives were held in slavery by their fear of death" (NIV). In Jesus' death and resurrection we find true significance, the courage to be vulnerable, and hope for eternity.

THE WAY OF THE DRAGON SLAYER

The Way of the Dragon Slayer: Seasoned Courage

In my first career as a social worker, I worked on a "family preservation" project in the rural town of Weed, California. Someone had referred a family to Child Protective Services after determining that the two parents were addicted to drugs and alcohol and neglecting their seven children, ages fifteen years old to sixteen months. My mission was to meet with this family twenty hours per week to provide counseling and supervise the safety and well-being of the children, with the goal of keeping the family together.

During my first week of visits to the family home, it was clear they were living in extreme poverty. Nine people shared three bedrooms, most of the glass was busted out of the windows, none of the toilets flushed, the kitchen was stacked with dirty dishes, and the only running water came from a hose that ran from an outdoor spigot through the kitchen window into the sink. Surrounding the house was a dirt lot crowded with about an acre's-worth of trash, junk cars, broken boards, plywood, bricks, cinder blocks, broken-down appliances, and bags of blankets and clothes. Some of the friends I grew up with lived in similar conditions, so this wasn't new to me. The bigger challenge was getting these nine people to let me help them. Things were a bit awkward at first, but after a couple of weeks it felt like we were starting to build some trust and rapport.

One morning during my third week of visits, I noticed something new as I approached the house—a huge stick, about five feet long, resting perpendicular to the concrete steps up to the front porch. I straddled the stick as I started up the steps, trying not to step on it and break my neck. I had just thought that I ought to remove this hazard by kicking it off into the yard when I heard the unmistakable sound of a rattle.

The next thing I knew, I was flying backwards off the porch, gaping in horror at what I now saw was not a "stick," but a full-grown, five-foot rattlesnake as thick as my forearm. I shuddered. That thing had been right between my feet!

Instinctively, I yelled, "Hey, everybody! Don't come out the front door!"

As soon as I did, I realized my yelling would probably have the opposite effect, and braced to hear and see seven children flood onto the porch. But no one came, and I soon realized there was no one home. How they got all nine people out of the house with no working car was beyond me, but somehow it had happened.

I spun on my heel and all but ran back to my car, anxious to vacate the premises. I had just reached for the door when a thought arrested me. *What if that thing bites one of these kids?*

It was all I could do not to panic. If there was anything in the world that freaked me out as a thirty-year-old man, it was snakes. I didn't even like seeing them on TV. I was a social worker wearing a tie, and I had never killed a rattlesnake in my life. And yet I knew with everything in me that I had to kill that snake to protect those kids.

The snake had now curled up against the front side of the house. Trying to keep my eye on it, I began to look for a weapon. Surely there was a shovel somewhere in all this rubbish. Making my way to the back of the house, I spotted one standing in a pile of dirt and tall weeds. It looked absolutely ancient. Cortez might have left it there in the 1600s. As I pulled it out, the handle wobbled ominously.

Clutching this Weapon of Death, I headed back to the front of the house. Waves of adrenaline coursed through me as I imagined the rattlesnake striking out at me from behind every corner. By the time I reached the porch, I was in a full sweat and felt like I was going to have a heart attack. To my slight relief, the snake was where I had left it, though it was starting to reach its head up toward the front door, which had a hole where a doorknob should have been. *Do not let that snake get in the house.* I began to concoct a plan to position myself on the porch and trap the snake between the door and the shovel. But the next moment, the snake changed directions and began sniffing with its tongue under the front window. Realizing I could now strike at the snake's neck stretched against the wall, I raised the shovel and began an internal countdown. *One . . . two . . .*

Before I could get to "three," a kitten suddenly dropped from behind the blanket acting as a drape in the front window. Utterly astonished, I took one look at the snake, who was now trained on the kitten, and knew this was what the snake must have been after all along. Lunging forward, I scooped up the kitten and flung it as far away as I could out into the front yard. As it scampered to safety, I raised the shovel again. Yet no sooner had I resumed my countdown when *another* kitten dropped from the window. *What is even happening right now?!*

I launched the second kitten into orbit, and the snake decided it was time to move. It took off toward the side of the house and soon disappeared into a huge pile of junk leaning against the fireplace chimney. With my Weapon of Death still clutched in one hand, I started to disassemble the pile, pulling away old bicycle frames, wood pallets, pieces of lumber, rolls of chicken wire, blankets, and rocks, all without any sign of the snake. Where had it gone? By now it had been twenty minutes since this whole thing started, and my heart was pounding so hard my vision was vibrating. Finally, I saw it, wedged behind two remaining cinder blocks from the junk pile.

All of a sudden, the snake's head reappeared, now with a cement foundation wall behind it. *One, two,* POW! I struck at his neck with the shovel like a panther. Immediately, the snake recoiled and began writhing violently behind the cinder blocks. *I got him!* I couldn't believe it. I had done it. I had actually slain the scariest thing I'd ever encountered. I had saved the lives of children! All I needed to do was to wait for it to stop moving.

A moment later, the writhing stopped and the snake's head rose into view again, not a mark on it. I had missed! What was I going to do now? I knew it probably wasn't going to give me another clean shot like that. I had to get closer and smoke it out of its hiding spot. Cautiously, I inched toward the cinder blocks, raising the shovel as I glimpsed the rattlesnake's scaled back. With a chopping motion, I brought the shovel down over the edge of the blocks, and that did it—the snake immediately slithered out into the open. This was it—the boss battle royale, *mano a snake-o*! High-stepping and chopping away, I finally got the snake's head under the edge of the shovel and jumped down on it with my full weight. I could feel its body slapping my legs for a moment, then fall lifeless to the ground, now separated from its head. It was over—for real this time. I had killed the snake.

Somehow I managed not to pass out. I found a white, five-gallon bucket, picked up the snake's body, and coiled it inside. It filled half the bucket. I then wrote a note warning the family that I found this on their porch, got in my car, and drove away. When I got on the freeway I could still feel my heart pounding. Eventually, I lifted both my feet up onto the seat of the car, just in case there was anything under the seat.

It took a while for the adrenaline to wear off, but the more I relived the experience in my mind, the more I felt a sense of wonder. I had just had my most direct confrontation with nature danger in my life, and it had provoked a kind of courage in me that I hadn't even known existed. Wow! If I could do something like that, what else could I do? My confidence and self-respect as a man grew about a foot that day, and have only grown since. In many ways, that was the experience that kindled my hunger for more encounters in the natural world, which ultimately attracted me to the adventures I've pursued in Alaska and other wild places. It's not a hunger for thrills—it's a hunger to see more of that courage rise to the surface in me. The greatest fuel for my self-respect has become proving that in the face of my own vulnerability, I can control myself to do what I didn't think I could do. This has become my definition of courage: *To command myself to face and conquer a fear that would otherwise leave me losing respect for myself.*

Over the last couple of decades I've met a few more snakes and found that they really don't bother me anymore. I live in the land of forest fires and rattlesnakes, and while I respect them, they no longer trigger my fight-or-flight reaction. When they leave me alone, I leave them alone, but when they endanger me or others I know how to deal with them.

I believe the courage to face nature danger lies in the heart of every man, which is why I was able to find it when the moment called for it, despite being well into adulthood before that moment arrived. But as I soon discovered, the best way to develop this courage—like all forms of courage—is to start hanging around other men who already have it.

Shain Zumbrunnen is another of my Alaskan hunting friends who seems more at home outdoors than indoors. He once told me he can't remember ever really being afraid in the woods—aware and respectful of danger, yes, but not afraid. "I think I'm more afraid of having a conversation with my thirteen-year-old daughter than I am of facing a wolf or a bear," he admitted. This is exactly the kind of man I want to go to the woods with, and thankfully he likes having me along, because I happen to know a thing or two about talking to teenage daughters and any other situation requiring relational courage.

One of the things that impresses me most about Shain is the way he is raising his children to be at home outdoors. I'll never forget when Shain told me the news that his son Peter had killed his first moose . . . at six years old. When I asked him how on earth he had trained a six-year-old to hunt moose, he explained that he had been taking his kids on hunting trips since the youngest, Sophia, was eighteen months and Peter and his twin sister Naomi were three years old. "I made the trips fun for them," Shain explained. "At that age it's just about making memories together, not teaching them to be hardcore." At first he just took them on short day trips hiking, fishing, or hunting—pretend-shooting with Nerf guns and warming up in the truck with their favorite snacks when they got tired or cold. But even on these fun trips, they started to build up their skills and endurance—especially Peter. By the age of four-and-a-half, his son was already showing remarkable stamina for trekking through the woods and weathering extreme temperatures, and had his heart set on hunting moose. Shain began teaching him to shoot a gun—first a pellet gun, then a .22, and even up to a 6.5 rifle. Finally, he took Peter out on his first hunt.

"I was most nervous about the things I couldn't really prepare him for," Shain told me. "The things that happen out in the field in a moment. So my focus was really on helping him stay calm and calculated so he could make a shot he felt good about."

Shain brought a friend with them, Travis, so one of them could walk Peter through his shot and the other could back him up if they wanted to get the kill. They came on five or six moose, and each time Shain walked Peter through the process of setting up, breathing, and deciding if he should shoot. Finally, they spotted a six-year-old cow moose grazing about a hundred and fifty yards away. Peter quickly turned to his dad and told him he felt good about making this shot. Travis agreed to help Peter breathe and count down while Shain got on his gun as backup. On Travis's count, Peter fired a perfect shot and the cow went down.

"It's an amazing experience seeing your kid, especially at such a young age, harvesting and supplying meat for your family," Shain told me. "Peter had such a huge grin on his face and he jumped right in to help us skin and cut up the moose to bring home."

Peter is now eleven and has put a lot more meat in the family freezer and trophies on the wall. Shain even took him to Africa on a hunting trip. This young boy can hold his own right alongside the most seasoned hunters, though he doesn't know that's a bit unusual for most American boys his age. It's less unusual for Alaskans, of course, because it's still part of the culture. Much of the population, especially in poorer communities, still subsists on what they harvest from the land—berries, fish, and game. The Department of Fish and Game issues educational hunting tags so school teachers can take entire classes out to the wilderness to learn how to hunt and process moose, deer, and other animals—they have a complete "field to table" curriculum. It's dinner conversation to discuss game and predator populations and to plan their lives around the harvest season.

Over the years I have loved bringing my family and friends to Alaska to hunt and spend time with Shain, Joe, Craig, and my other Alaska buddies because we get to be like Peter. We get to go into dangerous country and *have fun*. Without seasoned men guiding us through the process and teaching us how to regulate our nervous systems in the face of danger, hunting in Alaska would be terrifying, because we'd have much lower chances of making it out of the bush alive. Thanks to their training and courage, we not only survive but come out with thrilling tales to tell that keep us coming back for more.

The other thing I love about spending time with these men is observing their deep and cherished relationship with their land. Except maybe for those of us who still farm, hunt, and fish for a living, many of us in the "lower 48" never have the privilege of growing up with this kind of relationship with the land where we live. We don't fully appreciate the beauty and sustenance it gives us, and the responsibility it requires of us. We don't grow up understanding that we are cultivators and caretakers. But that is who we are called to be, and the best way to start stepping into these roles is to get around guys who have fully embraced them. Whether we live in the country or the city or work on the land or in a building, we are at our best as men when we are driven by humility, gratitude, awe, and love for the world our Father created and entrusted to us. This is where seasoned courage comes from—not from self-preservation, but from love.

ACTIVATE THE WAY OF THE DRAGON SLAYER

DEFINE THE DRAGON

Men are dangerous . . . but nature is dangerous too. Nature danger doesn't take you on personally. You are simply there at that time, in that place, and what happens there has next to nothing to do with you. The exposure of wide open spaces ignites a place in a man's heart of vulnerability and insignificance. Nature has a way of reminding a man that he is easy to kill. No amount of money, muscle or brains will hold up against what nature can bring whenever it wants to. The forces of creation humble a man before his Creator.

Nonetheless, God's intention for Adam in the garden was not to train him as an employee, but as a son who shared His love for everything He created, and through that love to become His partner in continuing to cultivate and care for the natural world and cause it to flourish. He thus led Adam on a journey of introducing Himself as Adam's Provider, Protector, and Connector, for only by receiving and learning from the source would he become who he was created to be. Our goal in our relationship with nature is to return to our role as a steward with a mindset to tend with diligent husbandry.

POINTS OF ATTACK

The most obvious level where we confront our fear of insignificance, vulnerability, and eternity is in our primal desire to escape the danger and discomfort of the natural world:

- "Accessing nature is too much work! I don't want to be that cold, hot, or dirty."
- "I can't imagine having to sleep out in the woods or on the ocean. It's too vulnerable and too wild!"
- "I've never had anyone who could introduce me to the wild. That first step feels too overwhelming and scary."
- "I hate being out of control so much that I've become an absolute control freak!"

LESSONS LEARNED

- Men need danger!
- To get out of our comfort zone, we need a "first time" again and again.
- Creation teaches us of the majesty of our Creator.
- Nature is beautiful but harsh—dig deep and Man UP!

THE SWORD

> Plead my cause, O LORD, with those who strive with me;
> Fight against those who fight against me.
> Take hold of shield and buckler,
> And stand up for my help.
> Also draw out the spear,

And stop those who pursue me.
Say to my soul,
"I am your salvation." (Psalms 35:1-3)

Finally, my brethren, be strong in the Lord and in the power of His might. Put on the whole armor of God, that you may be able to stand against the wiles of the devil. For we do not wrestle against flesh and blood, but against principalities, against powers, against the rulers of the darkness of this age, against spiritual hosts of wickedness in the heavenly places. Therefore take up the whole armor of God, that you may be able to withstand in the evil day, and having done all, to stand. (Ephesians 6:10-13)

Therefore, since [these His] children share in flesh and blood [the physical nature of mankind], He Himself in a similar manner also shared in the same [physical nature, but without sin], so that through [experiencing] death He might make powerless (ineffective, impotent) him who had the power of death—that is, the devil— and [that He] might free all those who through [the haunting] fear of death were held in slavery throughout their lives. (Hebrews 2:14-15 AMP)

Then God said, "Let Us make man in Our image, according to Our likeness; let them have dominion over the fish of the sea, over the birds of the air, and over the cattle, over all the earth and over every creeping thing that creeps on the earth." So God created man in His own image; in the image of God He created him; male and female He created them. Then God blessed them, and God said to them, "Be fruitful and multiply; fill the earth and subdue it; have dominion over the fish of the sea, over the birds of the air, and over every living thing that moves on the earth." (Genesis 1:26-28)

Then the LORD God took the man and put him in the garden of Eden to tend and keep it. (Genesis 2:15)

"You shall have no other gods before Me. shall not make for yourself a carved image—any likeness of anything that is in heaven above, or that is in the earth beneath, or that is in the water under the earth; you shall not bow down to them nor serve them. For I, the LORD your God, am a jealous God, visiting the iniquity of the fathers upon the children to the third and fourth generations of those who hate Me, but showing mercy to thousands, to those who love Me and keep My commandments." (Exodus 20:3-6)

HOW TO SLAY

1. Reflect.

    a. What level of engagement do you have with the environment around you? For the "avid indoorsman"—remember that your God is powerful, He is with you, He has called you, you are right where you belong, and He is able to work all things together for your good!

2. Connect.

    a. Describe your most recent or impacting experience with nature. Did it include something outdoors or indoors? How did that encounter recalibrate your sense of true significance, the courage to be vulnerable, and hope for eternity?

3. Adjust.

    a. Plan an overnight outside. Do it in your backyard if you need to!

b. Get to an ocean, mountain range, desert, river, or lake and take a walk around. Sit, listen, think and write down what you hear. What is God saying to you in what you see?

c. Wait for a great rain storm, put on your rain gear and work around the house, or just walk in the downpour. Feel the wind and wet on your face. Imagine you are on one of those boats on the TV show *Deadliest Catch*.

d. Jump on a snow machine or ATV and ride out into the wilderness for hours with some other guys. Ride your skill level, but be sure to push yourself enough to get an adrenaline dump in your bloodstream. Then gather up and talk about how "We could've died, but we didn't!"

e. If you have outdoor experience, invite another man who may not have done much outdoors and show him around the place!

CHAPTER 7
MAN AND MACHINE

If you ever have the privilege of visiting my friend Jon Fray's "man cave," you will quickly discern that this man is a master of flying machines. The man cave is actually attached to Jon's private airplane hangar. The small bush plane he flew to Anchorage every week for his twenty-eight-year career as a commercial pilot for Alaska Airlines sits inside, as well as another small six-seater plane he's rebuilding for fun. The runway outside gives him a great view of his beautiful house and property nestled in the mountains outside Big Lake, Alaska, which he and his wife, Kristie, built up from nothing over their twenty-four-year homestead.

Lining the walls of Jon's man cave are framed photographs. There's one of the airliner he flew for Alaska Airlines and another of the F/A-18 he flew for five years in the Navy before that, both covered in the signatures of his colleagues. There's also a series of sepia-toned photos from his childhood in Zimbabwe, where he grew up as the son of Southern Baptist missionaries. One shows Jon's father standing in front of a Land Rover, looking up at a small plane taking off. This was the first plane Jon flew in at eight years old, manned by a Missionary Aviation Fellowship (MAF) pilot. From that first flight, Jon knew he wanted to fly planes and be a missionary pilot. However, after pursuing this path for a number of years and encountering resistance and roadblocks, he began to consider that maybe God had a different path for him—one that still involved flying planes and helping people, but which looked different than the "ministry" he had grown up envisioning for himself. Over the years, his paradigm expanded as he saw that what mattered to God was him following his passion and using it to serve God and others.

While boys today grow up enamored by the idea of driving fast cars, flying planes or jets, or operating heavy machinery because it's "cool," Jon's passion for all things mechanical developed in a reality where a working Land Rover or small bush plane made a massive difference—often a life-or-death difference—in the lives of his family, their fellow missionaries, and the Zimbabweans they were serving. When Missionary Aviation Fellowship started bringing planes out to their remote location, it allowed them to bring doctors out to the villages every couple of weeks and reach areas previously closed off to them with the gospel. However, Jon also learned early on that if you were going to rely on machines, it was extremely important to know how to fix them when they broke down.

One memorable occasion that brought this lesson home took place when Jon was ten years old. Two or three times a year, his father took him and his two brothers on a day's drive out to a wildlife reserve to hunt so they could replenish their supply of dried meat. On one particular hunting trip, they were joined by a fellow missionary doctor and his boys. In the middle of their journey home, one of their Land Rovers suddenly quit working. Unwilling to abandon the vehicle in the bush, the two grown men went to work diagnosing the problem and soon determined that the fuel pump had gone out. Next, they began to innovate a solution. They removed the hood of the car and took the filter off the engine. Then they stationed Jon's thirteen-year-old brother on the front fender with a tin can full of fuel. His job was to slowly dribble the fuel into the carburetor to keep the car running.

Remarkably, they were able to progress slowly with this system for a few miles . . . until the inevitable happened. The car backfired, causing the fuel can in Jon's brother's hand to ignite. He reacted immediately, flinging the flaming can away from him into the tall savannah grasses lining the dirt track along which they were traveling. In a panic, the men and boys leapt from the vehicles, grabbing every blanket they could find and beating and stomping away to try to stop the fires that instantly sprang up wherever the burning fuel had fallen. Thankfully, they were able to keep the fires from getting out of control, and soon succeeded in extinguishing them.

After enjoying a moment's relief that they hadn't burnt down the countryside, they returned to the problem of how to fuel the Land Rover. What could they use instead of an open can? The doctor remembered that he had an IV bag of electrolytes in his medical kit. He pulled it out, emptied the liquid, refilled it with fuel, and threaded the tube down into the carburetor. He then instructed Jon's brother on how to use the sliding meter to control the flow of fuel into the car as he held the IV bag aloft. It worked! Refilling the bag as needed, they managed to drive the Land Rover for the remaining hours of the journey and get it home.

This experience and many others made a lasting impression on Jon. He learned firsthand that machines were wonderful but also dangerous, and that they needed men who could master them—convictions that have only deepened as he's watched cars, planes, and other machines become ever more complex, sophisticated, and effective throughout his lifetime. Though now retired, his passion for machines remains—especially those that fly—and he now shares it with his two grown sons, who both work with large machines (turbine engines and oil rigs). It's good to know there are men like the Frays managing the machines that get us from point A to B!

THE WAY OF THE DRAGON SLAYER

The Nature of the Dragon:
The Fear of Failure, Being Out of Control, and Death

Machines encompass every attempt man has made to expand his power through tools and technology. The word actually comes from a Greek root that means "to be able, to have power":

machine (n.)

> 1540s, "structure of any kind," from Middle French *machine* "device, contrivance," from Latin *machina* "machine, engine, military machine; device, trick; instrument" (source also of Spanish *maquina*, Italian *macchina*), from Greek *makhana*, Doric variant of Attic *mēkhanē* "device, tool, machine;" also "contrivance, cunning," traditionally (Watkins) from PIE *magh-ana-* "that which enables," from root *magh- "to be able, have power."[22]

Machines are what man builds as he gains knowledge of the forces, elements, and laws of the natural world and uses that knowledge to exert control over his environment. Water, fire, wind, and earth all have power, and harnessing these powers is one of the behaviors that separates us from the animals. The quest to find new technologies to accomplish our goals sits deep in our hearts. Men are always trying to put some kind of handle, seat, keyboard, combustion engine, or other device on raw power because we want to answer the question, "I wonder if we could get more power from this thing—what would it do?"

The history of man and machine is a tale full of trial and error exposing the truth that the power of our machines can be used for good or evil, to build or to break down, to save lives or take them. Men have built and used

---

22 | S. v. "machine," *Online Etymology Dictionary*, https://www.etymonline.com/word/machine#etymonline_v_2135.

guns to bring home meat for their families and defend their home from predators—and also as instruments of violence, murder, and war. The same internet technology by which we power our businesses and enjoy lightning-fast communication around the world today has facilitated human trafficking on a scale that dwarfs the African slave trade of a few centuries ago. Tools and machines can also backfire on us through faulty design or human error—the *Titanic*, the *Challenger*, and Chernobyl are a few epic examples. One Sunday, my friend and mentor John Tillery was working on building a house in the woods when the tip of his chainsaw caught on the wood and kicked back up in his face, slashing him from forehead to chin. I never fail to think of this each time I run my chainsaw and remember what the power in my hands is capable of.

While the Bible doesn't have much to say about *when* man began building tools and technology to harness the powers of the physical universe, it does tell us that when man decided to take knowledge outside of relationship with God, it inevitably became a project fraught with conflict, frustration, and fear. Genesis 3 introduces the idea that Adam's relationship with the natural world became "cursed," so that as he tried to master it through blood, sweat, and tears, it would essentially blow up in his face. Likewise when Cain murdered Abel, God announced that "When you work the ground, it shall no longer yield to you its strength" (Genesis 4:12).

The Bible also suggests that God had something to do with frustrating sinful man in his power-seeking technological pursuits. In Genesis 4, we see that after Cain became cut off from the strength of the ground, he went and built a city, and fathered a line of descendents who developed various tools, including musical, bronze, and iron instruments (see Genesis 4:17-22). Fast forward to Genesis 11 and we get the story of how a united humanity came together with their shared knowledge and technology to build a city and a tower "to make a name for [themselves]" (Genesis 11:4). In response, God nipped their grand plans in the bud by confusing their language, because "this is only the beginning of what they will do. And nothing that they propose to do will now be impossible for them" (Genesis 11:6). Apparently, a "hive mind" humanity bent on harnessing the powers of the world to build tools and structures to achieve divine status has always been a danger, and one God has ultimately prevented. This is what we should think of when we hear the word "Babel," which means "confusion"—God's commitment to frustrate our plans to take over the world with technology apart from Him.

However, sandwiched between the stories of Cain and Babel, we find God instructing a man to build a structure and even downloading the design specs and materials he was to work with. Noah, the righteous man of peace, built a "machine"—not to increase his own power or dominate the world, but to *preserve life*. Thousands of years later, we see God giving Moses blueprints for another structure. This time, it was the first prototype of God's dwelling with mankind—a project that will culminate, according to the book of Revelation, with a city powered by God Himself, the New Jerusalem, coming to earth. God also selected a man to build this structure, Bezalel, and "filled him with the Spirit of God, with ability and intelligence, with knowledge and all craftsmanship, to devise artistic designs, to work in gold, silver, and bronze, in cutting stones for setting, and in carving wood, to work in every craft" (Exodus 31:2-5 ESV). God, the true master of the powers of the universe He created, has always intended to partner with man filled with His Spirit to develop machines and technology that will preserve human life and build cities where God and man dwell together in unity. Tools and machines are part of how He designed us to take dominion and subdue the earth—to bring chaos into order. This is why the universe "waits in eager expectation for the children of God to be revealed. For the creation was subjected to frustration, not by its own choice, but by the will of the one who subjected it, in hope that the creation itself will be liberated from its bondage to decay and brought into the freedom and glory of the children of God" (Romans 8:19-21 NIV). There will be an end to the frustration between man and his mastery of machines—when he is no longer seeking to use his power from the wrong spirit, and is fully liberated through the Spirit of God to use that power as intended. And what is that wrong spirit? It is fear—the fear of failure, being out of control, and death.

THE WAY OF THE DRAGON SLAYER

Riding the Dragon: Who's in Control?

There's no question that in the context of human history, we live in a day of accelerated advancement in technology. Over the last three centuries, we have progressed from the agricultural to the industrial to the information age. With each decade, we have made our machines more sophisticated and complex, enabling many tasks and jobs formerly requiring significant time and manual labor to all but disappear from our daily lives, and opening up new jobs, fields, and sectors of the economy. We have built the tools and tech to power entire countries, map the human genome, discover quantum mechanics, send men to the moon, put access to the collected knowledge of humanity in our back pockets—and much more.

However, our machines have come with tradeoffs, many of which involve some serious downsides. The development of nuclear power—which many argue is the cleanest and most sustainable power available today—also gave rise to the nuclear bomb. Our world changed forever after we dropped the "Fat Man" atomic bomb on Nagasaki on August 9, 1945. It ended World War II, but started a new age of warfare. Now humanity is perpetually haunted by the specter of World War III or some other man made nuclear cataclysm that will blow up the world. Dozens of books, movies, video games, comic books, and other works of imagination have come out in the last eighty years depicting how tangible the threat of nuclear weapons remains in our minds. The atomic bomb epitomizes our collective fear that either through evil or error, men will use machines to annihilate ourselves.

More recently, we've been confronted with a spin on this fear—the fear that our machines will gain autonomy and either replace us, control us, or remove us from existence. Science fiction has been full of predictions about robots and artificial intelligence for decades—most of them dystopian. But now, automation, robotics, and artificial intelligence have reached a level of development where they are poised to (or have already) change or take over a vast number of jobs formerly done by humans. While many believe that this will be a net positive for the economy, the fear that we may actually soon be living in the world of *I, Robot, The Matrix,* or the *Terminator* has become part of our public conversations. In short, it seems that the greater our success, the more power and control we gain over our environment, and the better we get at improving and extending human life—some believe we will be able to extend it indefinitely—the more we are confronted by the potential for catastrophic failure, being controlled, and ultimately bringing death on ourselves through the machines we create. Advancing technology isn't slaying this dragon of fear, it's putting it on steroids.

With that said, most of us relegate these looming fears to the background of our awareness. Where this dragon really shows up is in our daily use of machines, where we are confronted with a catch-22. Apparently, the more sophisticated, smart, advanced, time-saving, labor-saving, and user-friendly our machines become and the easier they make our lives, the more we are in danger of becoming less smart, more dependent, and even controlled by them.

Consider the machine we all arguably use the most these days: the smartphone. This little device was supposedly created as a tool for greater freedom and connectivity. We have more news, entertainment, shopping, networking, banking, education, and business tools than we could ever use or consume right here in our hands and pockets. Yet this platform of seemingly infinite possibilities and empowerment has turned out to be a platform that also creates high levels of control, conformity, and disconnection. The problem is that our phones were basically designed as digital heroin. They addict us to an unending cycle of dopamine and cortisol hits to our brains, triggered by marketing, news, and entertainment appealing to our instincts for fear or pleasure.

In *The Ruthless Elimination of Hurry*, John Mark Comer lays out some alarming statistics about our relationships with our phones:

> A recent study found that the average iPhone user touches his or her phone 2,617 times a day. Each

user is on his or her phone for two and a half hours over seventy-six sessions. And that's for all smartphone users. Another study on millennials puts the number at twice that. In every study I read, most people surveyed had no clue how much time they actually lost to their phones.

A similar study found that just being in the same room as our phones (even if they are turned off) "will reduce someone's working memory and problem-solving skills." Translation: they make us dumber. As one summary of the report put it, "If you grow dependent on your smartphone, it becomes a magical device that silently shouts your name at your brain at all times."[23]

One of the dark realities behind this dependent relationship is that it is easily exploited by companies whose sole agenda is to take as much of our time, personal information, and money as they can. "Reminder: Your phone doesn't actually work for you," writes Comer. "You pay for it, yes. But it works for a multibillion-dollar corporation in California, not for you. You're not the customer; you're the product. It's your attention that's for sale, along with your peace of mind."

The uncomfortable truth is that if we are addicted to our phones (Comer recommends trying a twenty-four-hour digital fast to gauge just how addicted we are), then we are not in control—we are controlled. We are being directed by algorithms to point the resources of our life at a set of priorities determined by someone else. We are essentially plugged into the Matrix, living in a virtual reality while other forces use us to power their

---

23 | John Mark Comer, *The Ruthless Elimination of Hurry* (Colorado Springs: Waterbrook, 2019), 36-37.

agendas. In this condition, we are exceedingly vulnerable to developing a dependent, powerless mindset where we must rely on others to tell us what to think, what to feel, and what to do.

This danger isn't just coming at us from smartphones, of course. When I was growing up, most men I knew had enough mechanical skill to do basic maintenance and repairs on their cars. Now not only our cars, but everything from our vacuum cleaners to our fridges and toasters is "smart," which means if they break down, we either have to call in an expert or buy a new one. In general, the more our knowledge and technology has advanced, the more we have been conditioned to rely on others and "trust the experts" on how to do everything from dressing ourselves to managing our health, getting married, raising kids, and voting in the general election. But succumbing to this way of life and outsourcing our thinking, beliefs, choices, and behavior to others is the opposite of freedom.

The danger in today's world of machines is the same danger that has always existed—that by building tools to become more powerful, we will misuse that power. But as our tools become more powerful and effective, and become a ubiquitous part of the infrastructure of our society, that danger increases. Uncle Ben told Peter Parker, "With great power comes great responsibility." Dragon riders use the power of today's technology irresponsibly. The aggressive ones use it to control, dominate, or exploit others, and our machines now allow them to do it at an unprecedented scale. The passive ones—and I think the majority of us are tempted in this direction—use it to hand over responsibility for their lives to something else, also at a much greater scale than ever before. Many passive dragon riders are like the character Cypher in *The Matrix*. Tired of the danger, discomfort, and hard labor required to live and battle the machines in the real world, he is willing to betray his fellow freedom fighters to the machines just so he can return to slavery and have his body plugged back into the comfortable fantasy world of the Matrix. Like all addicts, the passive dragon rider is bribed and seduced by the "high" offered by machines and technology, and over time this becomes what he cares about more than anything else. He runs from the responsibilities of his life and is willing to sacrifice his resources and relationships to live in a world where he thinks he is master, but in fact is a slave.

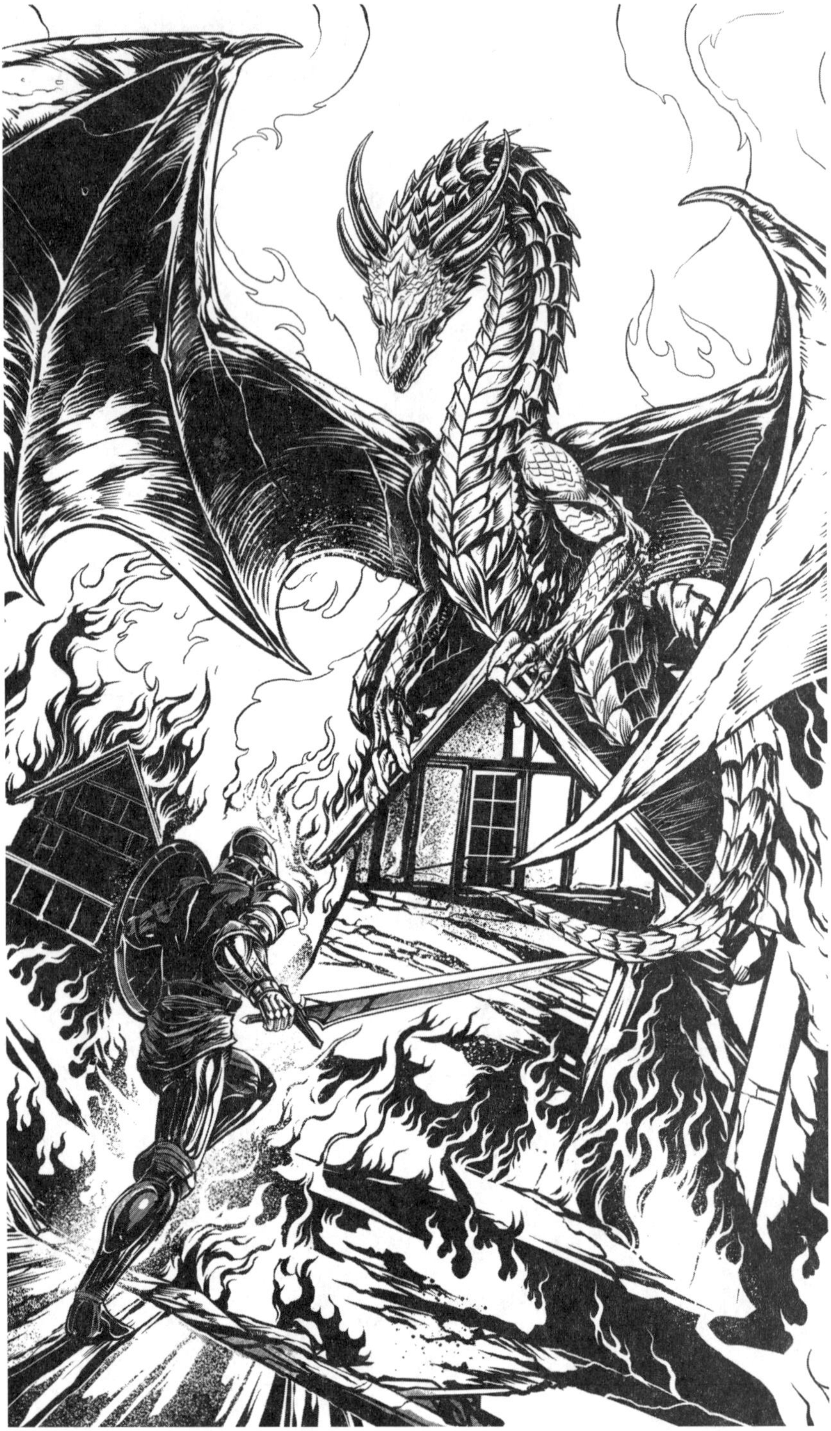

Facing the Dragon: Control Your Freaking Self

I remember at nineteen years old attempting the second rebuild of my 1965 VW engine. My goal was to increase it from forty horsepower and upgrade its overall performance. I had replaced everything—pistons, "jugs," distributor, camshaft, dual carburetors, manifold, and fan pulley—and given a cool paint job to all the sheet metal and fan housing. It was coming together like a work of art, and I was down to the finishing touches. Then I made a mistake. I was putting the distributor into the crankcase when I bumped the washer and it fell inside the crankcase (engine block). I couldn't believe it! How was I going to get the washer out of there without starting over and doing all the labor of splitting the case again?

That's the last thing I remember. The only way I can describe what happened next is that I went into a rage seizure. I lost my freaking cupcakes! I started throwing wrenches and kicking anything I could reach. I looked like an orangutan being attacked by hornets. I broke glass and bent metal and threw garbage up against the wall.

When I looked around at the damage, I felt stupid. I had made the whole thing worse and hadn't fixed anything. The washer was still in the crankcase. To this day, I still shake my head at my reaction to this incident. Did I really have such a hair trigger to things not going my way that I became a destroyer of everything near me? Was I lacking self control so severely that I wouldn't accept responsibility for my decisions? Was I really so immature that I could attack my own project in a fit of rage? Yup!

Even after I met Jesus at twenty-one, I continued to turn into the Hulk whenever I was dealing with tools, engines, broken bolts, or anything that didn't work right the first time. This uncontrolled rage was always primarily aimed at "things." I occasionally lost it with some people, but it wasn't common. When dealing with things, however, I was another person . . . and that scared me. Well into my Christian life, I was afraid to take on DIY projects because I didn't want that guy to burst out of me.

Thankfully, I grew up. Developmental psychologists claim that the prefrontal cortex—the rational, executive part of our brain capable of thinking through our decisions, weighing the consequences, and choosing to respond instead of react—doesn't finish developing until we're twenty-five or so. Just on that basis alone, I had a few years to wise up after the cupcake-losing incident. But more importantly, as I grew as a follower of Jesus, I learned to be led by His Spirit, and He began to produce the fruit of emotional and spiritual maturity in my life.

Galatians 5 is where Paul explains that the true nature of freedom is not license to do whatever our passions urge us to do, but is mature self-mastery through the power of the Holy Spirit. The ninth and culminating fruit of the Spirit is self-control (Galatians 5:22-23). Likewise, Paul told Timothy, "for God gave us a spirit not of fear but of power and love and self-control" (2 Timothy 1:7 ESV). As followers of Jesus filled with His Spirit, we have the greatest source of power—the power that made the universe—living inside us. Learning to access and use this power to master ourselves and mature to be like Jesus is how we become free men.

It was when I started learning to trust and use the power of the Holy Spirit inside me that I started to become a truly powerful person. I began to respond differently in situations that previously had made me feel powerless, like a failure, or out of control. I realized that was the problem when I came up against machines or tools that didn't work for me—they made me feel powerless, and I turned to the false power of anger (anger is often a mask for fear) to try to feel powerful. For some reason, more than the other dragons in my life, it was tools and machines that revealed my inner control freak. But the more I took on the identity, mindset, and practices of a powerful person, the less machines had the power to trigger that reaction in me. I began to master myself in the presence of machines, and the more I did so, the more courage I gained to work on mastering machines. This is the path to freedom for every control freak—control your freaking self!

As we've seen, the courage we gain by confronting the other dragons in our lives will equip us to face the ones we still need to slay. Overcoming my fears in my other relationships and roles—as a husband, father, leader, and adventurer in nature—called a level of courage out of me that made me feel more and more powerful and capable of taking on other challenges. Exposing myself to nature danger in particular gave me many opportunities to practice reframing my perspective from "I'm scared" to "I'm excited." Whether it was backpacking with my boys in the Trinity Alps or hunting deer on Kodiak Island, though I never experienced an attack or serious injury, my awareness that these could happen in a blink of an eye stayed at peak levels the whole time. But instead of interpreting this danger as a story in which I was a powerless victim—"I'm going to die!"—I chose to be in a story of adventure—"This is so exciting!" And one day, I decided to start doing the same thing with machines—especially with cars.

The man I am around cars today is completely the opposite of who I was at nineteen. I don't just love to drive them . . . I love to race them. I feel the need for speed! I am currently on a small race team that competes a couple times a year at two local race tracks: Sonoma Speedway and Thunderhill. We currently have two Porsche 944s and a BMW E36 and do a few types of races in the Lucky Dog and 24 Hours of Lemons (Lemons 24 for short) racing leagues.

Lemons 24 racing is the closest experience I have to driving a real race car. If you've seen the Netflix series *Formula One*, you have an idea of just how intense real car racing is. F1 is the ultimate in car racing because of the excellence of the machines. The epic sound of those cars ripping through your city is unforgettable. Two hundred miles per hour is no joke! The number of things that can go wrong at those speeds is incalculable and yet mere mortal men climb into those machines day after day. Why? Because that which doesn't kill you can thrill you!

Lemons 24 is admittedly a few steps down from F1 because we're not driving a McClaren around the track, but the intensity is like nothing else I have experienced. I tell Sheri that it is the most fun a guy can have with his clothes on! It is two, six-plus-hour days of endurance racing. The four drivers on our team take turns racking up three-hundred-plus laps in a weekend. Speeds down a straight may reach only half what F1 has going on, but the road track is mostly high speed turns. It is bumper-to-bumper, door-handle-to-door-handle adrenaline! The start of a race on a Saturday morning can have more than a hundred and fifty cars circling the two-and-a-half-mile track. I've seen Saturdays when the entire track is full of cars end-to-end before the green flag drops and the giant metal mosh pit ensues. Yellow flags are everywhere while guys work out their patience, skills, and frustrations. One by one, the weaker machines and drivers drop out, and by Sunday, only the strongest remain to race towards the checkered flag at sundown.

Of course, the drivers on our team aren't the only ones trying to master these powerful machines. We wouldn't be successful without our world-class mechanic, Louis Soros. Before each race day, Louis is the one getting the engine, power trains, brakes, wheels and tires, communication systems, driver feedback technology, pit supplies and tools, fuel dispensing apparatus, and driver safety gear in tip-top condition at his shop, EU Tech in Sacramento, California. His daughter, Renae, customizes our paint jobs and decal work, and gathers sponsors for free stuff and gadgets—including some water-cooled shirts that connect to an ice chest for those 108-plus-degree race days in California summers. Louis smuggled his family out of Hungary in the early 1970s from behind the "iron curtain." He and his wife and infant daughter went through a communist checkpoint lying in the trunk of a car. He told me how the trunk was filling up with carbon monoxide as the car idled in line. He pulled the rubber gasket out of the seal of the trunk to get enough air so that his family wouldn't suffocate. I'm not sure what you've done to get your family to freedom, but I've got nothing but love and respect for a man with the courage and determination to risk it all for them. He's the kind of man I want in my corner when I'm taking on my own risks with a car.

My journey with cars has convinced me that there is a sweet spot in man's relationship with machines, tools, and technology. That is simply the point where a man must exert enough energy to master himself and master the machine so that he feels the rush and satisfaction of solving a problem, conquering a challenge, and achieving a goal. I recently discovered that somewhere in Dubai, they've built a race track where they race F1 cars without drivers—they're fully computerized and driven through remote control. I immediately wondered why anyone would find this type of racing appealing. The whole experience and thrill of racing cars is that it brings man and machine together in a way that requires the man to demonstrate great skill, courage, and endurance. This is why we watch any sport, or anything involving humans performing at a high level. The minute we remove the human factor, we stop caring about it.

As men, we are always at our best when we continually force ourselves to live on the edge of discomfort, hard work, and risk, for that is the only place where our strength can grow. When we engage with machines in a way that pushes us to this edge, they become catalysts for us to expand and use our power to affect ourselves and those around us.

THE WAY OF THE DRAGON SLAYER

The Way of the Dragon Slayer: Learn from the Masters

We all use multiple machines every day. It's probably not realistic that we'll become masters of all of them, in the sense that we have the knowledge and skill to build or fix them. But we can learn to use them responsibly, and responsible use is the goal. Smartphones, airplanes, nuclear power, robots, and artificial intelligence aren't going away any time soon, and they need responsible, courageous men to master them so they become tools that can bring life and help the kingdom come on earth as it is in heaven.

Mastery is a learning journey. None of us starts out as a master—we start as novices, and if we stick with the journey, we progress to apprentice and journeyman before becoming masters. You've probably heard of Malcolm Gladwell's 10,000 Hour Rule—that's the average time investment of learning and practice it takes to master any advanced skill. This means we need to embrace the identity of a learner. And here's the beautiful thing—when you're a learner, failure is actually a required part of the road to mastery. I don't know who coined the phrase, but I repeat it often: "We are either winning or learning!" The way to overcome our fear of failure is not avoiding failure, but failing multiple times and learning how to do better. Failure is also the fertile ground for creativity and innovation. Most of the machines we use were created by men who failed repeatedly before getting it right, and they found the solution because they used their failures as fuel to drive them toward it.

So where should you start the journey to responsible use and mastery of machines? I recommend challenging yourself to identify one machine or tool you own that triggers this dragon of fear in you. Maybe it's your car or lawnmower. Maybe it's your smartphone. Maybe it's the chainsaw sitting in your garage. Maybe it's your pocket knife. (If you don't own a pocket knife, go get one!) Take one afternoon and intentionally engage with that tool or machine in a way that requires some effort and work. Try to set a goal—sharpening your lawn mower blades, changing your oil, doing a twenty-four-hour digital fast, fixing the clogged drain, or cutting that pile of logs out back. Then go to work. Watch a YouTube video if you need some guidance, or call a friend who you know is handy. Watch where you get uncomfortable and frustrated, and where avoidance behaviors or intense emotions arise. Invite the power of the Spirit to help you process these emotions, restore your calm and focus, and persevere in the process of learning and mastery.

From there, move on to a larger project—maybe something you can work on with a friend. Restore a car, build a tree fort, refinish a table, put together a little recording studio. If you are the handy guy, invite a few novices into your shop and mentor them in a thing or two.

Finally, I recommend that you find men like Jon Fray or Louis Soros—men who are masters of machines, and spend time with them. Ideally, try to arrange some kind of experience where they get to put their expertise on display for you.

I did just that for our first official Dragon Slayers trip in February of 2021. Nine of us gathered in Alaska—this time not to hunt, but to spend a week driving snow machines around the interior of the state. Our plan was to haul the snow machines to a spot five hours out of Anchorage, then drive them sixty-five miles out to a dog sledding lodge, from where we could make daily treks to explore the pristine, snow-covered country. What could go wrong, right? It was on this trip that I first quipped what has become a common refrain on our adventures together over the last few years: "We could've died, but we didn't!"

As on the Kodiak Island trip, four of the men were experts manning snow machines in Alaska, and the other five—Ben, Christian, Ron, Wes, and me—were from the "lower 48" and had rarely or never been on a snow machine in their lives. Craig, Shain, Jon, and Joe spent the first part of the winter months prepping the machines. To be specific, they bought three machines that didn't run and rebuilt them. I ended up with one of these machines that we dubbed "The Wounded Rabbit" because of the belt that squealed when I revved it up. Just that sound made me "wolf bait" as we traversed the arctic wilderness.

It is no reflection on the expertise of my Alaskan friends that these machines broke down in the most inconvenient ways in the most treacherous places—that's the reality of running snow machines in the dead of winter in Alaska. About twenty miles into our first leg of the journey, Ben's snow machine died on the trail. We all caught up to him and the Alaskans went to work to figure out the problem. A fuel line had failed and needed some "MacGyver" solutions to fix it—and they needed to figure them out quickly. Leaving the machine was not an option. The sun was going down and temperatures were dropping faster than the light was going out. We split the group and I led those with no riding experience into the outer darkness toward the lodge, which was still forty-five miles away. The experienced men stayed with the problem and, with frozen fingers and no daylight, stayed with the job until they found a solution. Hours after the first group found the lodge and warmed up, the second group joined the others, victorious and smelling of gasoline.

With all the machines in working order, we spent the next few days trekking through the screaming white landscape. For us non-Alaskans, this was extremely beautiful but also disorienting. The reason we kept going was because Craig Moseley was out in front. At one point we were riding on top of a frozen river that had water leaking up through the surface because of shifting ice. I knew we probably shouldn't be there, but we all trusted that Craig knew what he was doing. As a result, we reached another spectacular view of the Alaskan mountain range that hosts Mt. Denali and its indescribable majesty—all because we trusted Craig to go places we never would've attempted without him leading the way.

Being with men of this caliber, expertise, and gumption challenged us non-Alaskans to expect more from ourselves than we ever would have in these conditions. Each of us were pushed to our physical and emotional limits. At one point Ron, the biggest human I've personally ever stood beside, fell off his sled into seven feet of snow. After digging himself out, climbing back on the sled, and getting it going again, Ron was absolutely exhausted. When we got back from that day's ride, he said, "I think I burned up every freaking calorie in my body!" Our respect for the seasoned Alaskans grew by leaps and bounds as we appreciated their strength, energy, endurance, and skill for not just surviving but thriving in some of the harshest conditions on earth.

After each long exhausting day of riding these snow machines, we spent our evenings reviewing the most humiliating events of the day. Each man took turns weighing in on the other men's struggles, and every vulnerability shown that day was treated with hilarious laughter and exaggerated stories. In the process, we created a place of unconditional acceptance, a place where each man could be known in weakness, failure, incompetence, and humility. The bond we felt after these rib-cracking nights together was incredible.

As I reflected on the trip later, I realized that it had only been so successful because of two things. First, the non-Alaskans were willing to trust the Alaskans and ask for help when we needed it, and second, the Alaskans were good leaders. Each of us from the lower 48 knew we were making ourselves vulnerable by putting ourselves in a situation where our weaknesses and limits were bound to be exposed. In our normal environments, we don't often have to ask for help and usually try to avoid it. But when you have to ask for help or you might end up dead, it helps you take that risk of relying on another man. What really helps is seeing that you are surrounded by competent leaders who both can and want to help you. When we think of "alpha male" leadership, we tend to think of some special forces commander screaming out orders at his men or an NFL linebacker smashing his helmet into those he is wanting to inspire. But what most men need is someone who is paying attention to what his men need, and who demonstrates that his sole goal is to help them grow, conquer, and unlock the glorious potential hiding inside them. A good leader is courageous enough to go find out what his men need before they ask, ask for and give constructive feedback, and create the opportunities they need to be successful. The Alaskans were such leaders for those of us who were learning new horizons on this trip.

In the end, our time with these masters of snow machines brought home some truths about the benefits of being with competent, courageous, and virtuous men—Dragon Slayers—that I believe are universal:

1. *Dragon Slayers don't give up solving a problem.*
2. *Dragon Slayers must have other men to trust more than they trust themselves.*
3. *Dragon Slayers learn to be men by being around other Dragon Slayers.*
4. *Dragon slayers bond through teasing, laughing, and telling stories (enjoying each other).*
5. *Dragon Slayers need to learn to ask other men for help.*
6. *Dragon Slayers need a daring, humble leader.*

The snowmachine trip set a new bar for all of us—first in our value for each other as good men and brothers we could safely bond with, and second in our value for the kinds of experiences that only mastery of a skill or tool can create.

We live in a world full of manmade technology that needs to be mastered and managed by men, and a world full of problems that need solutions only men—in partnership with God and each other—will innovate and build. The tools we create can expand our power and effectiveness, but they are not the source of our power—that only comes from our Creator. It's on us to govern our machines through the power, love, and self-control of the Holy Spirit and use them responsibly to fulfill our design to protect, provide, and connect.

ACTIVATE THE WAY OF THE DRAGON SLAYER

DEFINE THE DRAGON

The history of man and machine is a tale full of trial and error exposing the truth that the power of our machines can be used for good or evil, to build or to break down, to save lives or take them. As technology explodes in our day and age, it is the heart of mankind that will determine the use and consequences of our discoveries.

When you ponder the possibilities of AI, robotics, cell phones, and a generation born into all this as their "normal," what do you see as the most important and urgent training we need to be giving our young men?

POINT OF ATTACK

- Fear of feeling stupid or getting hurt
- Triggering our inner control freak by failing to solve a problem
- Feeling vulnerable when are forced into learning
- Giving up and feeling defeated
- Experiencing shame when needing to ask for help

LESSONS LEARNED

- There is both satisfaction and danger in creating a solution.
- Want to be a control freak? Control your freaking self!
- We either win or we learn.
- Men don't give up solving a problem.
- Men must have other men to trust more than they trust themselves.
- Men learn to be men by being around other men
- Men bond through teasing, laughing, and telling stories (We enjoy each other!)
- Men need to learn to ask other men for help
- Men need a daring, humble leader

THE SWORD

> My brethren, count it all joy when you fall into various trials, knowing that the testing of your faith produces patience. But let patience have its perfect work, that you may be perfect and complete, lacking nothing. If any of you lacks wisdom, let him ask of God, who gives to all liberally and without reproach, and it will be given to him. But let him ask in faith, with no doubting, for he who doubts is like a wave of the sea driven and tossed by the wind. For let not that man suppose that he will receive anything from the Lord; he is a double-minded man, unstable in all his ways. (James 1:2-8)

> Then the LORD spoke to Moses, saying: "See, I have called by name Bezalel the son of Uri, the son

of Hur, of the tribe of Judah. And I have filled him with the Spirit of God, in wisdom, in understanding, in knowledge, and in all manner of workmanship, to design artistic works, to work in gold, in silver, in bronze, in cutting jewels for setting, in carving wood, and to work in all manner of workmanship. (Exodus 31:1-5)

For God did not give us a spirit of timidity or cowardice or fear, but [He has given us a spirit] of power and of love and of sound judgment and personal discipline [abilities that result in a calm, well-balanced mind and self-control]. (2 Timothy 1:7 AMP)

Honor all people. Love the brotherhood. Fear God. Honor the king. (1 Peter 2:17)

"A new commandment I give to you, that you love one another; as I have loved you, that you also love one another. By this all will know that you are My disciples, if you have love for one another." (John 13:34-35)

HOW TO SLAY

1. Reflect

    a. Are there DIY (Do It Yourself) projects around the house that you've avoided because you lacked the knowledge, expertise or the patience to attempt them?

    b. How many men do you have in your life who seem to have more mastery and be more comfortable with their level of danger in relationship with machines?

    c. If you are one of those men who are experienced in fixing things, riding things, or using power tools, have you invited other men into experiences where they might learn to improve their skills and gain confidence in those areas?

2. Connect

    a. Share and discuss with your brothers:

        i. Where you struggle most and want to grow in the area of self-control.

        ii. What skills, tools, or machines you want to master.

3. Adjust

    a. Do a DIY project around the house you've been avoiding.

b. Start a project with a friend that involves tools or machines.

c. Find a mechanic, handyman, or someone with skill and ask him to teach you how to do something with a tool or machine.

CHAPTER 8
MAN AND PROVISION

If you have ever spent time with a true entrepreneur, you've probably realized that this is a guy who thinks differently. The level of curiosity, creativity, and comfort with risk he carries around is just a lot higher than what the rest of us have going on. He has never seen a problem that does not look like an opportunity!

My friend Eric Knopf is one of these true entrepreneurs. He radiates positivity, humor, and creative solutions. He's the kind of man who seems so confident and secure, you might wonder if he has ever struggled with insecurity in his life. When you hear his story, however, you learn that while his entrepreneurial spirit is a gift, his confidence and skill as a builder of businesses has been forged through many tests.

The first and most important test in Eric's business journey came not from the marketplace, but his personal life. In college, Eric was hard at work developing his first entrepreneurial venture when he met and fell in love with a girl. This girl happened to come from a very prestigious family filled with successful doctors, lawyers, and professionals—but not many entrepreneurs. The general expectation in this family was that every member would go on to add letters after their name through higher education. This created some pressure for Eric when he decided to communicate to the girl's parents that he wanted to propose to her, and that his plan was to work full-time on his startup after graduation. They expressed some concern over Eric's ability to provide, for he was young and inexperienced, and becoming an entrepreneur is not known to be a safe, stable, and secure career path.

These concerns and expectations did not deter Eric from marrying the girl or pursuing his entrepreneurial plans, but they created an internal battle in Eric over his identity. He started hearing voices inside telling him he would not be good enough, and one day would lose it all and prove every fear right. He longed to win the approval of his family, but it was hard not to feel that approval could only be earned through certain financial success or academic accomplishment. Given this, Eric wrestled with whether he ought to get his MBA and a "real job." However, something inside him was committed to proving that he had what it took to be successful in building a business.

Eric certainly wasn't afraid of hustle and hard work. Knowing that nine in ten startups fail, he decided to launch multiple startups to increase his chances that one would succeed. Sure enough, most of them didn't survive, but a few of them did, and one was a home run—Webconnex, a software company that builds software for events, ticketing, and fundraising. After launching Webconnex in 2008, Eric and his cofounder, John, bootstrapped the company and grew it to forty employees and millions in revenue over the next decade.

The most important thing Eric did during those years building Webconnex was not to prove that he was competent as a businessman or a provider, however. He overcame his insecurity and chose to succeed for the right reasons. This happened in part because he made the crucial decision to allow another man to speak into his life. Early in his career, Eric started meeting with Dwight Hill, a Christian business mentor whose mission was helping Christian businessmen deal with the corrosive and corrupting influences they inevitably face. As Eric opened up about the concerns on his mind, Dwight quickly discerned that Eric's pursuit of business and financial success was tied to man-pleasing. One day, he flatly confronted Eric on this point. "You're driven to make money because you want to please your in-laws. Galatians 1:10 says that if you're still trying to please man, you can't be a servant of Christ. Pursuing money to please man is incongruent with your calling in the kingdom."

Dwight's words caused a personal reckoning in Eric's life. He realized that he had indeed been building his worth and identity on becoming the financially successful man who could win the approval of others. This sent him back to the Bible to repent and realign his heart and mind with the true foundation for his identity. He meditated on the reality that God was his Father, and he was a worthy and beloved son on the basis of that relationship and not his job performance. Colossians 3:23-24 became one of his guiding principles: "Whatever you do, work heartily, as for the Lord and not for men, knowing that from the Lord you will receive the inheritance as your reward. You are serving the Lord Christ" (ESV). He also latched on to the biblical principle of generosity as the key to keeping his heart free from the love of money.

This season of internal recalibration not only lifted the unhealthy pressure and insecurity off of Eric, it reset his priorities for building his business. Of course he wanted Webconnex to be profitable, but his bigger goal became developing the people and culture of the company. Thankfully he and John were on the same page with making Webconnex "a people company." They believed the best way to serve their customers well and build excellent products was to hire people of skill and character and then create a culture where everyone on their team could thrive. As the company grew, they invested in more opportunities for their team members to grow and connect, including "connection credits" for remote team members to travel and meet up with each other, and annual vacation trips where the entire team and their families could play hard, enjoy each other, celebrate their successes in the previous year, and get recharged to pursue new levels of growth in the year ahead.

In 2019, Eric and John took the Webconnex team on their most epic company trip yet. They rented an island in Belize (yes, an entire island!) for the Fourth of July and flew all their employees and their families out for a tropical vacation for a week. Life was at an all-time high for Eric—business was booming and his marriage, family, and faith were all thriving. By this time, Eric felt his successes had also earned him the respect and approval of his in-laws, though it had been a long time since he had looked to that as a measure of his worth. As he looked ahead to 2020, he had only excitement and anticipation for how the company would continue to crush their goals and grow. Little did he know that in a few short months, he would be facing the second great test in his business journey—the possibility of Webconnex's extinction.

In February 2020, the Slack channel Eric and his team used to keep tabs on their customers and the events market began to rumble with rumors of the COVID-19 pandemic disrupting public gatherings and events. A few customers with small events decided to postpone. Then the fatal blow struck. On Friday the 13th of March, the governor of California, along with many other governors around the country, officially canceled all public events and gatherings of more than a hundred people. Within hours, Eric watched his entire business evaporate. Webconnex's revenue model was to take a portion of event ticket sales and a payment processing fee. As each customer canceled their event, not only did the future ticket money disappear, the credit card company who handled the transaction included the processing fees when they refunded the customer. Within days, Webconnex's projected revenue dropped to nearly zero, and hundreds of thousands of dollars in fees that had already been paid to Webconnex were taken back by the credit card companies, decimating their cash supply.

There was no denying reality—things looked bad. Eric knew the pandemic could last for years. Their entire industry had been canceled and declared illegal—the way they had made money was officially banned by the CDC. There was no indication when public events would come back, or even if they would. No financial institution would offer them relief funding when they were doomed to go out of business. There was no weathering this storm—Webconnex was sinking and almost sunk. Eric's CFO crunched the numbers and delivered the news: they only had twenty-five days to keep the lights on.

In this moment, Eric heard an old, familiar voice trying to tell him he was a failure and that the naysayers had been right about him all along. He was going to lose it all, fulfill every fear and worst-case scenario, and finally prove that being an entrepreneur had always been a doomed dream. Other businesses were hitting a boom during COVID-19—why hadn't he chosen to go into one of those sectors instead of one easily destroyed by a pandemic? But he had already dealt with that dragon of self and knew his identity, and knew how to tell that voice to shut up. He had also slain the dragon that would try to tell him that this was some kind of punishment from God. He knew his Father was in his corner as his Comforter, Equipper, and Partner to build solutions and conquer any storm or attack sent against him. He just needed to lean in for the strength and strategies God would provide.

Instead of self-preservation, what Eric cared about most was the preservation of his family and his team. He began making whatever immediate adjustments he could think of to preserve cash and drop expenses. Knowing he didn't want to lay anyone off (which many of his competitors were doing), he began calling other companies and asking them if they could provide jobs for his employees. He also reached out to some trusted advisors for prayer, prophetic insight, and wisdom on what to do. The words he received didn't fully make sense at the time, but he immediately felt encouraged by them. One was about Isaac sowing in a famine and reaping a hundredfold, another was about David picking up five smooth stones to sling at Goliath, and the third was about dropping their nets on the other side of the boat. Eric understood that he needed to stay generous, find multiple ways to attack the situation, and begin looking at other niches in the market where their software tools could be effective.

After they were able to secure some payroll funding from the federal relief program, Eric and John called their team together on a Zoom call and laid out their plan.

"We're on a sinking ship," Eric explained to his employees. "But we're not going down without a fight. If you can go get another job, do it. We've lined up some opportunities for you with other companies. But if you want to stay, we're going to try to take some evasive maneuvers and we're going to fight like crazy."

Every single person on the Webconnex team decided to stay with the company. One guy simply said, "There's no sinking ship I'd rather be on."

Over the next few months, the Webconnex team built twenty-two new features that allowed their existing customers to use their software to resume their events, do ticketing for virtual events, and add waivers and other layers of security to their ticketing and registration process. They also "cast their nets" into a completely new niche and customer base. Agrotourism properties like pumpkin patches, corn mazes, and you-pick fruits and vegetable farms, which used to run primarily on a cash basis, were required to add contactless payments and registration during the pandemic so they could monitor the numbers of people on site. The Webconnex platform was easily customized for this need, and they began to attract these customers in droves. Instead of bringing in revenue from one 1,000-ticket event, these farms were seeing up to 1,000 registered visitors a day throughout the harvest season, which lasted for several months. A hundredfold increase indeed.

After the "we're going to fight like crazy" speech, Eric and John regularly posted a number where his employees could see exactly how many days they could stay alive with their current supply of cash. As they continued to work hard and innovate week after week, they celebrated as the number climbed from twenty-five days to forty, sixty, ninety, and six months. Then in September 2020, Webconnex set the highest revenue month they had ever seen as a company. In October, they doubled that number, and in November, they matched October. By the end of 2020, they were up almost ten percent in annual revenue from 2019.

Since 2021, Webconnex has only continued to grow. They now have over one hundred employees and process over two billion dollars in payments each year. The innovations to their software tools developed during the pandemic have continued to help them serve their customers, and to attract more. They were also able to use their profits to attract a private equity partner so that when another pandemic-level crisis comes along, they won't be fighting for their existence. In the end, they emerged from the storm of 2020 as a stronger, more united team, and a more resilient business positioned to grow and succeed for decades to come.

As for Eric, the testimony of what God did to bring him, his family, and Webconnex through the pandemic has forged an unshakable confidence, gratitude, and hope in him. After watching so many friends and colleagues struggle and even flounder in their faith in the midst of this crisis, and plenty of business owners go into self-preservation mode and sacrifice their people to try to save themselves, he understood how crucial it was that he had already done the work to get established in his identity so he didn't implode or go back on his own principles when the storm hit. Instead of being crushed and demoralized, he was able to lean in and partner with his Father to build creative solutions that benefit thousands of people—his immediate family, his employees, their customers, and their customers' customers. He trusted his Provider when it mattered most, and his own ability to provide got a massive upgrade.

THE WAY OF THE DRAGON SLAYER

The Nature of the Dragon:
The Fear of Lack, Limitation, and Comparison

A provider is more than a guy who brings home the bacon. The word "provide" comes from the Latin *pro* + *videre*—to "see ahead" or "to have foresight." A man who provides is first and foremost a man with a vision. He looks into the future and discerns what is necessary to prepare for that future or make it happen. He is a creator and dreamer who imagines possibilities, and devises plans and strategies to realize them. Like a scout, he ventures out into the unknown ahead of others so they can anticipate whatever dangers lie ahead and take the safest path. He sees what he must do today to be ready for tomorrow.

The role of provider was baked into God's design for man from the beginning, because Adam was mandated to rule, subdue, and take dominion. His Creator gave him a truly great vision—conquering the wild, untamed world and establishing order through which it could flourish and be fruitful. And in Adam's case, everything he could possibly need to be successful in executing this vision was already fully provided for by his Father. Before God ever put Adam in the garden, He planted fruit-bearing trees there for his sustenance. He also walked with Adam each day, training him to see the design and potential of the natural world so that he could learn to provide what it needed to thrive. Adam did not start in poverty, but with the great abundance of his Father at his disposal as he was groomed to manage the family business.

When Adam took the fruit of the forbidden tree, he was taking the one thing the Father had said was *not* provided for him. The dragon deceived Adam into believing he needed something the Father had said was off limits. He sowed doubt in Adam's relationship with his Provider, convincing him God was withholding something good from him. In betraying his Provider, Adam compromised his own role as a provider. The nature of deception is that it darkens and distorts your ability to see. Through his fall, Adam's vision became distorted by fear, guilt, and shame, and provision became a struggle.

Exiled from the place where his every need was met and he was free to focus fully on his work of creativity and cultivation, he now had to work for his survival, and with a new awareness that his time on earth was limited. Without sensing the backing of the Father's favor, abundance, and safety as he once did, and with certain death in his future, how could he help but feel unsure that his own needs would be met, much less confident in his ability to meet the needs of others and the world? Now, instead of being able to create a legacy of generation after generation building wealth, knowledge, and diverse skills to fulfill the original vision, the men of Adam's race would inherit his insecurities and turn the role of provider into a competition with winners and losers. Thus entered the ancient weakness that has long plagued man's heart in his role as a provider—the fear of lack, limitation, and comparison.

THE WAY OF THE DRAGON SLAYER

Riding the Dragon: Who Benefits?

"What does a man do? . . . A man provides. And he does it even when he's not appreciated, or respected, or even loved. He simply bears up and he does it—because he's a man."[24]

These sound like the words of a father exhorting his son to do his duty to his family. In fact, this line is spoken by a drug lord in the third season of the hit television show *Breaking Bad* as he attempts to persuade the main character, Walter White, to return to his previous side hustle cooking meth. At the beginning of the show, Walter is a fifty-year-old high school chemistry teacher who turns to drug-making after learning he has stage-three lung cancer and less than two years to live. Desperate to provide for his wife and two children, one of which is disabled, he decides to use his chemistry skills for this dangerous, illegal, and lucrative purpose. It does not go well, of course—murder and mayhem ensue, and eventually his wife finds out what he is up to and wants a divorce. At the threat of losing his family, Walter decides to retire from the drug business. Yet after this speech by the drug lord, he falls back into his life of crime. As he becomes entrapped further and further in the world of deception and violence where he will meet his doom, Walter's tragic flaw and the truth of his motivations are revealed. He has told himself that the noble end of providing for his family justifies the ignoble means of the drug trade, when in fact he has become addicted to the adrenaline, ego inflation, power, and wealth it brings him. Only after he has ruined everything in his life and is facing certain death does he admit to his wife, "All the things that I did . . . I did it for me. I liked it. I was good at it. And . . . I was alive."[25]

Many of the aggressive dragon riders in the realm of provision are like

---

24 | *Breaking Bad*, Season 3, Episode 5, "Más," Written by Moira Walley-Beckett, Directed by Johan Renck, Aired on April 18, 2010 on AMC, https://www.youtube.com/watch?v=9-eQU4kw4Q4.

25 | *Breaking Bad*, Season 5, Episode 16, "Felina," Written and directed by Vince Gilligan, Aired on AMC on September 29, 2013. https://www.youtube.com/watch?v=FMb7TcArrZE.

Walter White. They don't all end up doing something illegal to make money, of course (some do). In fact, many of them invest their time, skills, and energy in careers that society views as perfectly respectable, if not noble. They become leaders in medicine, government, business, entertainment, and even philanthropy. They gain wealth, power, influence, and favor—and those in themselves are not necessarily evil things. The problem is that as they work to achieve success and climb the ladders in their respective fields, the goal of self-benefit becomes entrenched in their whole *modus operandi*. Success becomes defined by the experience they are creating for themselves, not for those they are positioned to influence and serve. They believe they can overcome lack by accumulating more, limitation by bending the rules, and comparison by establishing a fortified position at the top. And so they make small compromises because the ends justify the means. They become toxic, critical, manipulative, and narcissistic as they use people and work to subdue or eliminate their rivals. They excuse and avoid taking responsibility for mistakes or harms caused under their leadership, and purposely build a lack of accountability into their leadership culture. And the whole time, they are telling themselves and the world that what they're doing is acceptable, necessary, and right.

Often surrounding and enabling these aggressive dragon riders are passive men who are benefitting from them. They may be shareholders of their companies, consumers of their products, their spoiled children, or even ministry leaders who want their tithes and financial support. A passive dragon rider doesn't really care about being productive. Instead of developing his talents, resources, and opportunities and creating something of value, he exerts his energies to get other people to provide for him. Like the aggressive dragon rider, he is looking out for his own benefit, but instead of hustling to build his own wealth, he wants to live off the wealth of others. He is a parasite. He uses his lack, limitations, and resentful comparisons to others to justify playing the victim and build a case that he deserves to be taken care of.

Unfortunately, both of these dragon riding styles have become entrenched in our society over the last four or five decades, as evidenced by two trends—the expansion of the wealthy and poor classes while the middle class has shrunk, and the rise of the culture of entitlement.

While wealth creation in itself isn't evil, most members of the wealthy class today don't appear to be focused on using their wealth to benefit others. For example, of the $42 trillion in new wealth created in 2020-2021, two thirds were captured by the super rich—in a time in which most of the world was losing work, income, and resources due to the policies of the COVID-19 global pandemic.[26] This was in part because companies that profited greatly from the pandemic policies (Walmart, Amazon, etc.) decided to use their profits to reward their shareholders, most of which belong to the wealthy investment class, rather than using it to raise wages for their workers or keep prices low for customers. That decision didn't come out of nowhere, of course—it had been the expected practice of large corporations, stockholders, banking institutions, and our government for decades. The "haves" look out for themselves and apparently, they never have enough.

Meanwhile, the attitude of entitlement has become more and more prevalent in our culture. Over the last century in the United States, we have shifted from being a nation that valued saving and investing in hard assets like land and property to a nation of borrowing and spending. Most people trying to "keep up with the Joneses" are leveraged to the hilt, and so are the Joneses. We also once believed grit, hard work, and determination were our best solution to overcoming poverty, but since the sixties we have become an ever-expanding welfare state in which more and more people depend on "entitlement" programs. Our national debt is now in the tens of trillions because we encourage people to live off the government and pass the problem of how to continue funding these unsustainable programs on to our children and grandchildren. One effect of this borrow-and-spend culture is the "failure to launch" problem among the Millennial and Gen Z generations,

---

26 | Samantha Fields, "How the world's richest people became much richer during the pandemic," *Marketplace.org*, January 6, 2023, https://www.marketplace.org/2023/01/16/how-the-worlds-richest-people-became-much-richer-during-the-pandemic/

where young people prolong staying dependent on their parents, rack up massive student loans and other debt before they even start working, and express frustration and resentment on social media when their first job or salary doesn't enable them to support a comfortable middle-class lifestyle.

Sadly, a culture where people are not just allowed but encouraged and incentivized to look out for their own interests before the interests of others is a culture where corruption, injustice, and lawlessness flourish. This is exactly what we are seeing in our culture today, and there's only one thing that will turn the tide. It isn't rioting or more regulation—we have seen how those, like anything else, can become captured and used as tools by self-interested men. It certainly isn't putting our heads down and continuing with business as usual, hoping it will all work out somehow, for if we do that, we are contributing to the problem. Albert Einstein said, "The world will not be destroyed by those who do evil but by those who watch them without doing anything." Our only hope is for more Dragon Slayers like Eric to rise—men who have conquered their fear of lack, limitation, and comparison and are living intentionally as the apostle Paul instructed: "Do nothing from selfish ambition or conceit, but in humility count others more significant than yourselves. Let each of you look not only to his own interests, but also to the interests of others" (Philippians 2:3-4 ESV).

THE WAY OF THE DRAGON SLAYER

Facing the Dragon: Upgrading Our Vision

"You give them something to eat" (Mark 6:37).

Thousands of people had trekked into the wilderness to find Jesus and sit at His feet. The disciples probably thought they were being compassionate when they came to Jesus and urged Him to send them away to buy food for themselves so they wouldn't starve. In response, He gave them this challenge—"You provide for them."

The disciples only knew one way to provide food for a multitude—lots of money. They did the calculation and came up with a number—feeding that many people would cost about two-thirds of an average person's annual income. Again, Jesus' response broke their brains and their categories. He took the little food they had, blessed and broke it, and had the disciples hand it out to the people, who "all ate and were satisfied" (6:42). Notably, there were twelve baskets of leftovers—one for each of the disciples. They got to provide and be provided for.

Jesus was inviting His disciples into the realm in which He lived—a realm without lack, false limitations, or unhealthy comparison. It is the realm of the Father's abundance, from which every need in the human experience can be fully satisfied. Jesus wanted His men to be the ones to feed the people, because He wanted them to understand that they, like Him, were sons of the Father and had access to all that was His. Over and over, He told them what the Father was like—that it was His pleasure to give them the kingdom, that He already knew what they needed before they asked, and that the Father loved them so much that He would even send His own Son to restore them to their place as sons. As Paul asked, "He who did not spare his own Son but gave him up for us all, how will he not also with him graciously give us all things?" (Romans 8:32 ESV).

But for a long time, the disciples didn't get it. Even after participating in two miraculous multitude feedings, they got stressed when they thought Jesus was upset at them for not bringing bread on one leg of their travels.

This prompted a strong "brotherly shove" from Jesus: "Do you not yet perceive or understand? Are your hearts hardened? Having eyes do you not see, and having ears do you not hear? And do you not remember?" (Mark 8:17-18). It's sobering to realize that you can experience and even do amazing miracles with Jesus and still be blind to what He's trying to show you. But it can happen because our ability to see is connected to the state of our hearts. A hard heart resists change, while a soft heart is open to letting Jesus fundamentally mess up and reconfigure our identity, how we operate, and our vision for life.

I first heard this in my involvement with Promise Keepers:

> "A man without a vision is a man without a future—And a man without a future will always return to his past!"

We all know those guys who were great high school athletes and then fizzled out, never left their hometown, and still long for the "old days." But this saying applies to many men—even Christians—who are living without a compelling vision for their lives that aligns with their God-given identity, design, and purpose. This is what the Bible is referring to when it says, "Where there is no vision [no revelation of God and His word], the people are unrestrained; But happy and blessed is he who keeps the law [of God]" (Proverbs 29:18 AMP). The word "unrestrained" means "to let the reins loose." When you drop the reins on a horse, it will stop completely, run wild, or eventually mosey back to its feeding trough. Its great power becomes undirected and unchanneled toward any purpose. The same is true of us—without a divine vision to direct the energies of our lives, we stall out, burn out, and revert to what is familiar, even if we know we're settling for less than what is available to us. As my friend Ron Adkins once wisely observed, "A man doesn't know what he wants—he wants what he knows." And for most of us, what we know is the reality of lack, limitation, and comparison. Even as Christian men, our vision for what it means to be providers is often defined more by our past experience and the world around us. This is why our relationship with money and other resources is typically a dance of worrying that we'll have enough to pay our expenses and hoping we have enough to indulge in some creature comforts. This falls so short of how we were created to live.

One of my favorite verses is Psalm 32:8-9:

> I will instruct you and teach you in the way you should go; I will guide you with My eye. Do not be like the horse [or] like the mule, [Which] have no understanding, Which must be harnessed with bit and bridle, Else they will not come near you.

God doesn't want to "rein" us in, He wants to direct us with His "eye"—His vision for our lives. Jesus came for this purpose—to show us the Father, how He sees us, and how He wants us to relate to Him. Through signs and miracles of healing, deliverance, multiplying food, raising the dead, walking on water, calming storms, and finally through His sacrificial death and resurrection, Jesus showed us a Father who desires nothing more than to create an experience for us in which we feel seen, accepted, loved, cared for, nourished, and blessed. The resources of His kingdom are pointed toward our benefit. He is our Provider.

But Jesus also showed us that the Father wants more for us than simply to receive His provision. We all need miracles of provision in our journey with God, because it leads to secure trust and attachment with Him, just as a baby forms a secure attachment with his or her primary caretaker when the caretaker responds to the baby's needs. But from that secure place, He wants to lead us on to maturity, which is becoming a generous provider who looks like Him. True victory over the fear of lack, limitation, and comparison happens when we not only start to practice generosity and seek the benefit of those around us, but when we discover—as Jesus was trying to show His disciples—that our role as providers is to be stewards and distributors of the Father's resources. We are not the source of provision, we are the managers.

This was the lesson God was trying to teach Israel in their journey to the Promised Land. In the wilderness, they experienced miraculous provision every day and were fed with the "bread of angels." This was solely to establish their relationship with God as their Provider. But all along He was leading them to a land with "large and beautiful cities [they] did not build, houses full of all good things [they] did not fill, hewn-out wells [they] did not dig, vineyards and olive trees [they] did not plant" (Deuteronomy 6:10-11). They went straight from daily manna to stewarding the cultivated wealth the Father was giving to them as an inheritance, specifically because God did not want them to say, "My power and the might of my hand have gained me this wealth." Rather, He wanted them to remember it was He who gave them "power to get wealth, that He may establish His covenant which He swore to [their] fathers" (Deuteronomy 8:17-18).

When our vision for provision is to be a steward, manager, and generous distributor of our Father's wealth, it changes everything. It sets us free from striving to conquer lack and limitations (which are often more false perception than reality) and leads us to experience levels of mastery, influence, success, and blessing we simply can never experience when we are tripping over the need to benefit ourselves first. It enables us to give our focus fully to our *metron*—the set of skills, talents, resources, relationships, and responsibilities we are individually assigned to cultivate and tend. Nothing breaks off the fear of comparison like understanding that each of us has been entrusted by God with our own realm to manage, and that He chose it for us "according to our abilities" (see Matthew 25:15). As long as we are giving ourselves fully to that assignment and vision, we can be sure that we will lack nothing to be successful. We just have to access what the Father has already made available to us.

Seeing ourselves as stewards also awakens our creativity and dreaming. As we discussed in Chapter 2, when we believe we're a loved son in the living room with our Father, and not a criminal in a courtroom before a judge, we live a life marked by both discipline and dreaming God-sized dreams. Dreams give us focus for our discipline, and discipline enables us to accomplish our dreams—but we also need the awareness of the Father's abundance and our stewardship role to keep our dreams and discipline rooted in the framework of vision. This is how we discover that the dreams of our heart were actually designed by God to not just bring us fulfillment, but to benefit others. Every dream in your heart, whether it's to master the guitar, start a business, travel the world, write a book, have a family, coach or pastor people, lead a revival, or whatever it may be, is ultimately a dream about you creating something with your life that can bless and benefit others. And guess what? That's exactly what the people in your realm of influence and responsibility—and the world—need.

THE WAY OF THE DRAGON SLAYER

The Way of the Dragon Slayer: Building Your Legacy

Around the time my friend Charles Kown got engaged to his wife, Robyn, she told him she had always wanted to adopt a child. He was open to the idea down the road, but as it wasn't an immediate decision they were making, he didn't give it a lot of thought. They got married and began having children of their own. Then, after their second son was born, Robyn broached the subject of adoption again. She said she felt it was a good time to start the process, and Charles agreed to look into it with her.

Robyn was specifically interested in adopting internationally, so they began to research various countries and continents, including Russia, Africa, and China. After praying, they both felt like they should pursue adopting a child from China. They were particularly drawn to this after learning that China had high numbers of orphans due to the country's longstanding one-child policy. Many Chinese parents were forced to either abort or surrender their children after having their one allowed child. Due to parents favoring male children, baby girls were more frequently placed in orphanages, and many babies requiring medical care were surrendered by parents who couldn't afford it.

As Charles and Robyn began seriously discussing the prospect of adopting a little Chinese girl, potentially one with health problems, Charles approached this decision in his usual analytical manner, weighing the pros and cons and counting the cost. International adoption is an expensive, time-consuming, and emotional process, and at the end of it you have a child who will need lots of love, help, and healing as you raise them to adulthood. It's not a decision one makes without careful consideration and commitment.

When his analysis didn't help him arrive at a firm conclusion about whether they should move forward with the adoption or not, Charles called a friend of his who had already adopted a child from China and took him out to lunch to get his advice. After hearing Charles lay out all his concerns, the man looked at him and simply said, "I think you're asking the wrong question. Instead of asking why you should do this, ask, 'Why shouldn't I do this?'"

This question shifted Charles' whole paradigm and ended up making what had seemed like a tough decision clear and straightforward. As he looked for reasons why they shouldn't adopt, all he could come up with was that he was scared of the unknown. He knew right away this was not a good enough reason—his entire life had been a journey of trusting God and stepping into the unknown, particularly in his career in finance. He had left secure, high-paying jobs and moved his family to different states following God's invitation to step out with Him into the unknown. He had learned that the safest and best place to live was on the edge of faith and risk. Well, this was another situation where he now recognized that God was calling on his courage and inviting him to partner with Him in something new. *God calls us to take care of those in need,* he reasoned. *I have the opportunity and urge to adopt an orphan in need. God is with me and this is His heart. Why wouldn't I do this?*

From that point on, Charles was fully on board and engaged in the adoption process with Robyn. That didn't necessarily make the process easy—it was still long, arduous, and costly. But feeling secure and settled that this was the right decision turned it into a journey of trust and hope that as they did their part, God would do His part to provide all that was needed. After spending months establishing their eligibility to adopt, they finally received a referral for a child—a six-month-old baby girl with congenital femoral deficiency (CFD) in her left leg. They then had to wait nearly a year after accepting the referral, during which they had to apply and wait for all the immigration paperwork to be approved, before finally bringing their little girl, Mamie, home.

Of course, finalizing the adoption was just the first stage of the journey. The Kowns knew from the moment they said yes to adopting Mamie that they were in for a long and difficult road trying to help save and repair her left leg so it could develop as normally as possible. They found a specialist in Baltimore, Maryland who could treat her, and began flying up regularly from Alabama for him to help her left femur grow out to match her right leg. Thankfully, she has made steady progress in a positive direction. Now thirteen years old, Mamie is continuing to receive expert medical care and physical therapy, and is on the road to being able to walk and run on two full-grown healthy legs.

This is what it looks like to be a provider with the heart of the Father. We use our resources to raise the quality of life for those God has entrusted to our care. For Charles, that includes a child from the other side of the world. For Eric Knopf, it includes his family and the one hundred employees at his company. It's a different group of people for all of us, but our job is the same. We invest in seeing them grow, mature, become whole, and flourish. Is it hard work? Absolutely. But as Charles discovered, once we settle in our hearts that this is what God is asking us to do, the hard work becomes worth it and we can fully and courageously give ourselves to it, confident that we will see Him provide all that is needed along the way.

In his instruction to husbands, Paul tells us to "nourish and cherish" our wives in imitation of Christ's love for the church (see Ephesians 5:29). "Nourish and cherish" goes much further than paying the bills and keeping a roof over someone's head. When you cherish someone, you provide for them because you are investing in them for the long term. The way you love them and impact their life for the better is going to be your legacy to the coming generations and into eternity. Some of these investments might be smaller gestures—giving them encouraging words, buying their favorite gifts, or taking them to places they enjoy. Some might be more significant, like supporting them as they pursue their dreams and develop their talents, perhaps paying for their education or connecting them with an amazing sports coach or music teacher to train them. And sometimes you make big sacrifices to supply their needs and put them in an environment where they can thrive. Whether big or small, when we cherish people by upgrading their experience in life, we are investing in our generational and eternal legacy.

Of course, investing in people means paying attention to what they need, how they receive love, and what causes their eyes to light up. My wife's top two love languages are Acts of Service and Quality Time. I've learned that if I walk around the house with a drill, hammer, and ladder fixing things that Sheri needed done while listening to her talk about her day, I might just end up with her wrapped around my body later that evening! Why? Because she feels the laser of my provision and skill pointed at her as her man. That's right, she responds with her heart to me using my hands to improve her environment. I am built to provide that experience for those around me.

Implied in this is that we can and should also be investing in ourselves to provide for others more effectively. When we do the work to get emotionally, physically, and spiritually healthy, master useful skills, manage our finances well, and cultivate hobbies, it should overflow into blessing those around us. For example, in my youth I worked as a meat cutter. A couple decades later, I fell in love with grilling meat for people and started investing in the training, equipment, and ingredients to become a grillmaster. Grilling involves so many things I personally enjoy—fire and smoke, delicious meat, and the chemistry, physics, timing, style, and daring involved in preparing and cooking meat to perfection. But the best and most rewarding part is feeding people well!

In the end, the path to becoming the providers we were created and called to be is simple:

1. Identify the people God is calling us to serve with our lives.
2. Learn what they need and how best to meet those needs.
3. Develop the skills, acquire the resources, and make the sacrifices necessary to meet those needs.

If we truly give ourselves to these three things, we won't need to worry about our own needs being met. Remember the twelve baskets of bread and fish the disciples picked up? It's part of the deal—when we faithfully steward the wealth of our Father's house and generously give to others, He always shares the provision with us.

Lastly, as with all the dragons, we need our brothers to grow into the providers we are created and called to be. I didn't grow up with a father who modeled provision, but men like John Tillery, Bob Hasson, Eric Knopf, Charles Kown, and others have all brought their strength, skill, and expertise in stewarding resources into my life. As a result, I have been able to provide my family, Loving on Purpose, and the people we serve with an experience I never would have been able to provide on my own. When you get around true providers who live to bring benefit to others, their maturity, security, and generosity will help cast out the fear, lack, limitation, and comparison! Like Jesus, they carry the awareness of the Father's abundance wherever they go. These are the men who model the way we were designed to live—as men full of hope, joy, energy, and readiness to serve because we are connected to the realm where there's always enough.

ACTIVATE THE WAY OF THE DRAGON SLAYER

DEFINE THE DRAGON

Voltaire said, "Don't think money does everything or you're going to end up doing everything for money."

When our vision for provision is to be a steward, manager, and generous distributor of our Father's wealth, it sets us free from striving to conquer lack and limitations and leads us to experience levels of mastery, influence, success, and blessing we simply can never experience when we are tripping over the need to benefit ourselves first. We use our resources to raise the quality of life for those God has entrusted to our care. We take responsibility to tend to the garden, field, or *metron* of our lives, which God gave us "according to our abilities." We care for and love people and we steward, consume, and use the things. We never get that part mixed up!

POINTS OF ATTACK

- I have failed to plan and now I am living my failure. This is hopeless!
- I am a slave to the tyranny of the urgent. I don't have any time to think about tomorrow.

- I am a slave to the lender!
- I will spend my time now building a better future for my family and I'll spend time with my family later.
- I have one more investment to make and then I'll take care of my relationships.

LESSONS LEARNED

- Wealth is for my use in nourishing those around me.
- My life is a catalyst to infuse benefit into my *metron*, relationships, and community.
- I am in partnership with my Father as a steward of hope, strength, encouragement, resources, and His kingdom on this earth.
- Identify the people God is calling me to serve with my life.
- Learn what they need and how best to meet those needs.
- Develop the skills, acquire the resources, and make the sacrifices necessary to meet those needs.

THE SWORD

> Then God said, "Let Us make man in Our image, according to Our likeness; let them have dominion over the fish of the sea, over the birds of the air, and over the cattle, over all the earth and over every creeping thing that creeps on the earth." So God created man in His own image; in the image of God He created him; male and female He created them. Then God blessed them, and God said to them, "Be fruitful and multiply; fill the earth and subdue it; have dominion over the fish of the sea, over the birds of the air, and over every living thing that moves on the earth." (Genesis 1:26-28)

"For the kingdom of heaven is like a man traveling to a far country, who called his own servants and delivered his goods to them. And to one he gave five talents, to another two, and to another one, to each according to his own ability; and immediately he went on a journey. Then he who had received the five talents went and traded with them, and made another five talents. And likewise he who had received two gained two more also. But he who had received one went and dug in the ground, and hid his lord's money. After a long time the lord of those servants came and settled accounts with them.

"So he who had received five talents came and brought five other talents, saying, 'Lord, you delivered to me five talents; look, I have gained five more talents besides them.' His lord said to him, 'Well done, good and faithful servant; you were faithful over a few things, I will make you ruler over many things. Enter into the joy of your lord.' He also who had received two talents came and said, 'Lord, you delivered to me two talents; look, I have gained two more talents besides them.' His lord said to him, Well done, good and faithful servant; you have been faithful over a few things, I will make you ruler over many things. Enter into the joy of your lord.'

"Then he who had received the one talent came and said, 'Lord, I knew you to be a hard man, reaping where you have not sown, and gathering where you have not scattered seed. And I was afraid, and went and hid your talent in the ground. Look, there you have what is yours.'

"But his lord answered and said to him, 'You wicked and lazy servant, you knew that I reap where I have not sown, and gather where I have not scattered seed. So you ought to have deposited my money with the bankers, and at my coming I would have received back my own with interest. So take the talent from him, and give it to him who has ten talents.

'For to everyone who has, more will be given, and he will have abundance; but from him who does not have, even what he has will be taken away. And cast the unprofitable servant into the outer darkness. There will be weeping and gnashing of teeth.'" (Matthew 25:14-30)

"So husbands ought to love their own wives as their own bodies; he who loves his wife loves himself. For no one ever hated his own flesh, but nourishes and cherishes it, just as the Lord does the church. For we are members of His body, of His flesh and of His bones. "For this reason a man shall leave his father and mother and be joined to his wife, and the two shall become one flesh." This is a great mystery, but I speak concerning Christ and the church. Nevertheless let each one of you in particular so love his own wife as himself." (Ephesians 5:28-33a)

The rich rules over the poor,
And the borrower is a servant to the lender. (Proverbs 22:7)

There is one who scatters, yet increases more;
And there is one who withholds more than is right,
But it leads to poverty.
The generous soul will be made rich,
And he who waters will also be watered himself.
The people will curse him who withholds grain,
But blessing will be on the head of him who sells it. (Proverbs 11:24-26)

HOW TO SLAY

1. Reflect.

    a. Who is a man you know who models generous provision and focuses on bringing benefit to others with the resources of his life? How does he inspire you?

b. Consider your metron. Who and what are yours to steward? What is your plan to add strength and courage to these people? What is your plan to be diligent and effective in the use of your time, skills, talents, and resources?

2. Connect

   a. Open up with your brothers about your fears and struggles with provision. Invite them to share insight, wisdom, and encouragement to help you upgrade your vision for who you are called to be as a provider.

3. Adjust

   a. Ask your wife what she needs from you that you can provide.

b. Ask God to show you a person or situation who would be blessed by your time, energy, resources, or finances in some way and then give it to them.

CHAPTER 9
BILLY'S TWELVE

As I contemplated the subtitle for this book, various options came to mind—*Seven Fears Every Man Must Conquer, The Seven Battles that Make a Mature Man, Seven Keys to Becoming the Man God Created You to Be*, and so on. In the end, there was one that best captured the heart of the Dragon Slayers message: *Seven Reasons Men Need Brothers*.

As we have seen, having true brothers in our lives—not just men we hang out with, but men who have access and permission to challenge, sharpen, and strengthen us because they love us—is not optional on the journey to become a mature man and a Dragon Slayer. It is essential. This is why each "Activate the Way of the Dragon Slayer" section requires you to connect with other men in your life as you face these fears and master these areas of relationship and responsibility.

But I want to do a lot more than simply tell you to find and cultivate your band of brothers. In this chapter, I want to show you how I have been building my own band of brothers, share my plan for building momentum and culture around this model, cast vision for how a rising generation of Dragon Slayers can turn the tide for men over the coming decades, and hopefully inspire you to join this movement.

Meet the "OGs"

As I explained in Chapter 1, hearing Wm. Paul Young's account of Billy Graham expressing regret that he hadn't chosen twelve men to pour his life into sparked my conviction that that was exactly what I needed to be doing in my life. I understood that Billy was talking about making a covenant with twelve men and giving them priority access to his time, energy and resources. Billy realized that the way we change the world is by walking with men throughout our lives—not just in discipling relationships, but in covenant relationships. Jesus Himself, after three years of training His disciples, announced that He was promoting them from servants to friends. Before He went to the cross, He washed their feet and made a covenant with them, commemorated by the ritual symbols of His broken body and shed blood. His ultimate goal for the men in whom He had chosen to invest His time, attention, and energy was for them to transcend the rabbi-disciple level of relationship and to enter the deeper intimacy, love, and sacrifice of covenant friendship with Him and with each other.

Covenant is where we get to experience the strength of brotherly love—not just in a moment, but over a lifetime. But it also demands that we commit to offering the same strength in return, which is why many of us stop short of making that commitment. And so we end up with what Stephen Mansfield calls "rusty relationships." We allow the distractions of our busy, transitory lives to keep us from establishing consistent rhythms of connection with many important people in our lives. We may experience periods of feeling close with a friend, but when circumstances change, the connection grows distant. If we later reconnect with him we hear ourselves saying, "No kidding! Has it really been five years since we talked?" Covenant relationships only work when we are intentional about cultivating and protecting our connection in every season and circumstance of life. It is only through this consistency that we find and form those friendships that "stick closer than a brother," especially in times of difficulty or weakness when you need them most.

The first thing I did when considering which men I would choose to make a covenant with was to pray and ask the Lord for wisdom. There were dozens of amazing men I knew and could have chosen. But, I knew this group was supposed to be different, strategic, and something that could be replicated. After much thought and prayer, I came up with ten criteria—I call them the "Billy's Twelve Ingredients"—that would guide my selection process:

1. This is a man you enjoy.
2. He wants your influence in his life.
3. He wants to change the world.
4. He wants to grow.
5. He will commit to this group.
6. He agrees to take responsibility for twelve other men.
7. He agrees with the creed.
8. He wants to be accountable.
9. He has a generational mindset.
10. He has a covenant heart.

You've already met all the men I ended up choosing in the pages of this book, but let me tell you how the selection process unfolded. The first men I introduced the Dragon Slayers concept to were my guys in Alaska—Jon Fray, Craig Moseley, Joe Huston, and Shain Zumbrunnen. These four men had been present for each of my significant hunts. We'd spent many hours in "nature danger," around campfires, and on eight-hundred-mile drives together. I'd been in their homes and some of them had been in mine. All my family members knew them and most had been on adventures with one or more of them leading the way (Sheri is the only remaining holdout—maybe we can get her on a fishing trip someday). I knew each of them to be a man of great character, capacity, and experience. They had spoken into my life and allowed me to speak into theirs.

I also brought in the men I spent the most consistent time with. I lived with my son-in-love, Ben Serpell, worked with Christian Zamora at Loving on Purpose, and talked with Bob Hasson a few times a month if we weren't hanging out somewhere in the world together. These were the guys who called me out the fastest, encouraged me the most frequently, and knew by the look on my face how things were going on inside me.

Next, I reached out to Ron Adkins and Wes Kotys. I originally met both of these men on ministry trips—Ron on a visit to the prison in Texas where he was helping with their school of ministry, and Wes at church conferences in Valparaiso, Indiana, where he served as a church board member. Wes had also joined me for multiple hunts in Alaska.

After getting these nine guys on board, I officially launched our Dragon Slayers group in the fall of 2020, as I described in Chapter 7. Our plan was to meet on a monthly Zoom call for five months and then gather in Alaska for our first Dragon Slayer adventure—the epic snow machine ride into the Alaskan Interior. On our Zoom calls, I began to share the vision of knitting men together for the long haul. We also talked about how scary and exciting it was going to be to do something half these guys had never done before, and that whatever happened, we were going to walk away knowing each other more, with some good stories to tell. As the date of the trip neared and our anticipation grew, nervous laughter and teasing began to dominate our calls. Bonding was underway, and as I have already described, it just got better and better throughout the trip. During those evenings at the dog sledding lodge, after we rehashed the day's adventures and laughed till our sides ached, we began to dip into deeper and more personal waters. We talked about the seven dragons, how each was impacting our lives at that time, and what it could look like for a band of brothers to walk together for the rest of our lives. These conversations were informal and barely structured, but I learned things about these men—most of whom I had known for years and some for decades—that I'd never heard before. We were raw, vulnerable, and fully present with each other. It was an experience that brought us all to the same place in our hearts and it happened so deeply and quickly.

When I got home, I pondered who I could add to this group who would meld easily and well. Eric Knopf, Charles Kown, and Allen Cardines, Jr. all came quickly to mind. They met all the nine criteria on the list and were simply some of the most stellar human beings I had ever met.

Of course, I soon realized I was probably building this team in a less than ideal manner. I had gathered a collection of men who I knew and who knew me, but apart from a few exceptions, didn't really know each other. Most of them didn't live anywhere near one another, either. I would've made it much easier on myself if I had just gathered a group of friends from church who already knew each other and would more quickly reach the levels of trust and vulnerability required to truly relate as brothers. Nonetheless, I loved these men and felt confident that they would be open to connecting with each other. I had created a setup and challenge for myself to demonstrate my commitment to this group—to be the hub of relationship who, over years, would consistently make a place for them to gather and connect to me and each other. I understood and embraced that my faithfulness to fulfill that responsibility would set the bar for all the covenant relationships in the group.

We resumed our monthly Zoom calls following the Alaska snow machine trip and brought in Eric, Charles, and Allen. Our conversations were lively and exciting, and everyone was on board with what we were there to do. We initially focused on casting a vision for the culture we wanted to build within the group. We agreed that our mission was twofold—to build a band of brothers and raise up an army of fathers to heal a generation of orphaned sons. We also designed and completed the Dragon Slayer creed, which I shared in the first chapter:

DRAGON SLAYERS CREED

Men always protect
They never exploit the weak

Men always set the standard of love
They never hate their enemy

Men always provide resources, strength, and identity
They never consume or compromise the quality of life for others

Men always control themselves from the inside out
They never control other people

Men take full responsibility
They never blame others or neglect their responsibilities

Men sacrifice for the benefit of others
They never sacrifice others for their own benefit

Men live submitted to other men
They never live as the masters of their own universe

Next, we began getting to know each other better by having each man tell his story. One by one, each guy unpacked his life and the others asked questions and commented. This ended up taking up much of our time together that first year, but it was worth it to build the foundation of relationship together. We also tried to organize another Alaska trip, thinking that we could shove a river float trip into that first summer, but it was too much too soon. About half the group was able to make it out to South Dakota for a pheasant hunting adventure in November of that first year, however. We had a great time and Charles and Ron got to meet each other.

As we headed into our second year, I began to experiment with different approaches to how to spend our time together on the Zoom calls. As I was still developing the content for this book, my first plan was to ask each of the men to take turns answering these four questions:

- What's your "Dragon's Head"? (Area of combat this month)
- What's your God story? (Tell us how God is leading you)
- How are you adding strength to those around you?
- Who are you convincing that you love them? (Who are your targets?)

I used this template more as a playbook for running the calls. I allowed the conversations to roam freely and give each man ample time to speak, but I knew where to refocus the group if we needed it. I also made sure to nudge any of the guys who seemed more quiet and withdrawn to jump in and participate, tacitly reminding them that openness, vulnerability, and support were the experience we were pursuing together.

I also began to introduce the idea that my vision for Dragon Slayers was that each of the twelve men in our group would find twelve men to start a group of their own. If our mission was to build an army of fathers, this was how we were going to reproduce ourselves and recruit good men to join the movement. I didn't give them a time frame or pressure them to start the group before they were ready, but I explained that this was how they would transition from just being a brothers in our group to the father of their own group, taking on the responsibility to be the keeper of the covenant flame and hub of relationship for others. I encouraged them to use the same "Billy Twelve Ingredients" when selecting their men and reminded them that this was a marathon, not a sprint. Cultivating genuine covenant relationships is the work of years, not days or weeks. But if each of us was successful in forming our own band of brothers and giving them the tools to go out and do the same, the dynamic of multiplication would kick in pretty quickly.

Christian created this graphic to help visualize that the "army" we were talking about was completely possible to build twelve guys at a time over just a few generations of Dragon Slayers:

GENERATIONAL DRAGON SLAYERS

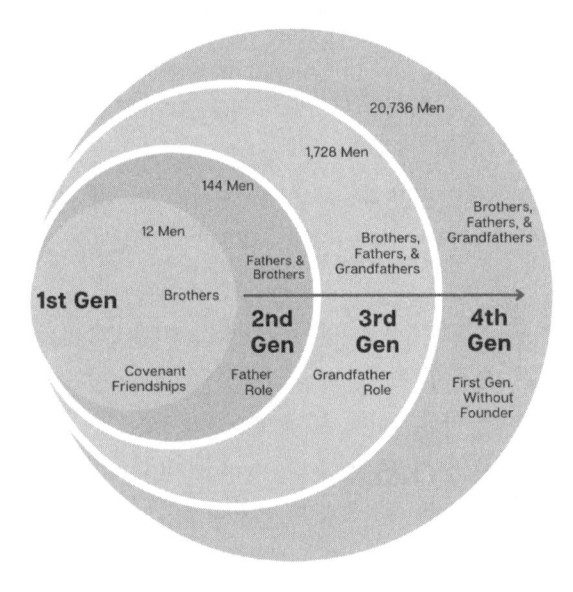

Generation	Men	Role
1st Gen	12 Men	Brothers / Covenant Friendships
2nd Gen	144 Men	Fathers & Brothers / Father Role
3rd Gen	1,728 Men	Brothers, Fathers, & Grandfathers / Grandfather Role
4th Gen	20,736 Men	Brothers, Fathers, & Grandfathers / First Gen. Without Founder

Just four generations out, we're looking at over twenty thousand men joined as brothers and fathers, slaying the dragons of fear in their lives and rising up as protectors, providers, and connectors in their spheres of influence. If those men reproduce themselves, the number jumps to 248,832. A generation after that, it jumps to almost three million men. By the seventh generation, it's in the tens of millions, and by the eighth, it's 429,981,696—far more than the entire population of the United States. I know these numbers might seem too big to comprehend or unrealistic, but this is how any significant trend or influence spreads through a community, nation, and around the globe. As Malcolm Gladwell explained in *The Tipping Point*, movements don't need to reach the majority of a population before they become "epidemic." You just need a small group of dedicated people who are doing and communicating something compelling and replicable—he calls it "sticky"—and it will take off.

Ben and the "2Gen"

Of all the guys in my group, which I now call the "OGs"—Original Gatherers—the one most ready to run with the goal of building his own Dragon Slayers group was my son-in-love, Ben. His experience on the snow machine trip (and the earlier trip where he and Craig killed the bear) allowed him to taste "brotherhood" like he never had in his life. When his snow machine broke down, he got to be on the receiving end of a group of men who would not quit until they solved the problem and, without exaggeration, saved him from death on the tundra. It's the closest thing he'll probably get to what injured or trapped men in battle experience when their fellow warriors rescue them because they "never leave a man behind." He also felt what it was like for other men to trust him and believe in him. When the Alaskans stopped to fix his snow machine, Craig threw Ben the keys to his sled and said, "Take mine and we'll catch up to you." In that moment and the one when they faced a charging bear together, Ben got to hear a skilled, seasoned man tell him, "You have what it takes to do what is needed right now." As someone who lives with this guy, I've gotten to see firsthand how much the confidence Ben walks in as a man, husband, and leader has grown because of these interactions.

Ben was also deeply affected by how real and raw the men became with each other on that trip, and by the level of connection he felt with all of them even after just a few days together. One of the key concepts I introduced to the guys at the beginning of Dragon Slayers was that our goal was forming healthy "soul ties" with each other. If you've gone through any kind of inner healing ministry, you may be familiar with the idea of "ungodly soul ties" (modern psychology might call them "trauma bonds" or "fear bonds") that need to be broken and cleansed so we can recover from past wounds and toxic relationships that are tripping us up. Not enough time gets spent, in my opinion, on teaching people how to build healthy, godly soul ties with other people. The first example of a godly soul tie in Scripture is the covenant friendship between Jonathan and David: "Now when [David] had finished speaking to Saul, the soul of Jonathan was knit to the soul of David, and Jonathan loved him as his own soul" (1 Samuel 18:1). A healthy soul tie is a heart-to-heart connection characterized by love, trust, and safety.

Two primary things are necessary for forming godly soul ties:

1. Time spent together
2. Healthy vulnerability

These are the purpose for our monthly calls, and especially for the Dragon Slayer trips, which is why it was a priority for me to get one in the books for our group during our first year. As I've said, there's just something about taking a chunk of dedicated time away from the rhythm of our normal lives, sharing in some kind of physical challenge, and then sitting down at a hunting lodge or around a campfire together that invites men to open their hearts to one another on a deeper level. The conversations Ben had with the guys on that trip allowed him to talk about painful emotions and struggles and receive their acceptance, encouragement, and wisdom.

Ben's first year in Dragon Slayers sealed the deal for him—his life was better for having these brothers in it, and he wanted to start creating that experience for other men in his life he knew and loved. He began recruiting and soon had twelve guys on board. Like the OGs, his 2Gen group was a mix of guys who lived near and far, some who knew each other and some who just knew Ben. He went to work casting the vision for the group, building out a twenty-four month plan for their monthly calls, and leading them through the journey of first getting to know each other and then getting in the trenches to slay dragons and grow together.

Right from the beginning, Ben boldly told his guys, "The goal of this group is to build covenant relationships. I am committing to walk with you for my entire life. I am committed to your well-being and to staying connected to you. I don't know what you are going to do, but that is my commitment to you." Initially, some of them pushed back on the "covenant" concept. They understood the idea of having a covenant with their wife, but applying that to friendships with other guys was foreign to them. How did it work and what was it supposed to look like, especially when most of them lived far away from each other and couldn't really "do life" together?

The most important thing Ben did in response to this was to demonstrate that—thanks to the powers of modern communication technology—it was actually possible to create a safe place where these guys could consistently be vulnerable with each other and build connection and accountability. A humble leader with a pastor's heart, Ben took the lead in showing his men what was going on inside him and inviting them to do the same. He had no need to dominate or take up all the air in the room, and was gentle but courageous in challenging his men to be truthful and calling them when they showed fear, cowardice, pride, or irresponsibility. He also borrowed a tool from our friend Jason Vallotton, founder of BraveCo, called "battle buddies." He paired up the guys in his group and explained that they were responsible to check in with their buddy once a week. His goal was to help the guys go deeper in getting to know one another outside of their monthly calls together and start to pull on one another's strength.

Ben knew his plan with his guys was working when, months into their journey together, he called one of his guys who he knew was struggling with some things in his life. When he asked how things were going, this man started telling Ben how he had talked to his battle buddy and several of the other guys in the group and they had all been helping him tackle his problems. As more months unfolded, similar situations arose that proved to Ben that his guys were truly showing up for each other in life and not just on a monthly call. For example, one of Ben's guys was driving a friend's car across the country and got in an accident that totaled the car. He called Ben to tell him about the situation and ask him to pray. Ben put out the word to his group and within two days, they had pooled almost a thousand dollars to send to their friend.

Now a couple of years into their journey together, some of Ben's guys are starting to gather their own group of guys to lead. In June of 2023, we held our first Dragon Slayers gathering at The Refuge in Wyoming with seven members of our OG group and seventeen guys from 2Gen groups and the 3Gen groups they have started—we filled that lodge with twenty-four men in total. One evening as we were all gathered around the dining room table sharing our experiences with the Dragon Slayers journey so far, one of Ben's guys got up with tears in his eyes and shared that he had been hesitant to commit to a group like this or believe it could really work because of men who had hurt him in the past. His experiences with the Dragon Slayers had convinced him that covenant relationships with men could actually exist and that they were exactly what he had been missing in his life. Other men chimed in to echo his sentiment.

As I watched moments like this and other powerful interactions unfold on that trip in Wyoming, I thought, *It's happening.* Dragon Slayers is still very much in its foundation-building years. Full disclosure—I have yet to have a monthly call where at least one of the OGs couldn't make it, and the twelve of them still haven't all met each other in person! But the covenant soul-tie building is happening, and with it I see courage rising in each man's life to slay their dragons. As the prophet said when the foundation of the restored temple was completed, "Do not despise these small beginnings" (Zechariah 4:10 NLT). What gives me the most hope and confidence is seeing that so many men are hungry—even starving—for brotherhood. They just don't know where to find it or how to build it. As great as many men's movements have been in the past, many of them have emphasized big events, gatherings, and discipleship over learning to build and walk in covenant with other men. Dragon Slayers exists to help men forge these vital friendships.

Find Your Twelve

There's a scene in the film *The Untouchables* where Sean Connery, who has been ambushed by the assassins of Al Capone, is bleeding to death. In his dying breaths, he turns to Kevin Costner, who plays the righteous crusader Elliot Ness, and asks, "What are you prepared to do?" He is calling Ness to take off the gloves and go after the evil and corruption that has gained a deathgrip on the city of Chicago. His words provoke Ness, who has been weary from the long battle against Capone's organized crime network, to dig deep and recommit to doing whatever it takes to dismantle the network and bring Capone to justice. Ness ultimately succeeds in this mission.

What are you prepared to do? It's not a coincidence that the brotherhood of men has been corrupted, attacked, and even decimated in our society and that at the same time, institution after institution has become hollowed out, perverted, and destroyed, from the family to education, medicine, entertainment, finance, business, technology, government, the judicial system, and even our churches. Somewhere along the line, the connections between fathers and sons and brothers and brothers were broken, and the traditional pathways by which boys become initiated into manhood "deconstructed." An African proverb states, "If the young men are not initiated into the village, they will burn it down just to feel its warmth." As we saw in Chapter 1, things are "burning" wherever we look. Family breakdown. The mental health crisis and rising suicide rates. Widespread porn addiction. An epidemic of obesity and chronic health problems. Drug and alcohol addiction. The loneliness epidemic. The list of signs and symptoms that the men of our society are lost, self-destructing, and hurting the people around them either by their aggression or passivity could go on and on.

Forget all these macro problems—just take stock of the men in your life. Are they thriving and living with a mission? Are they courageously pursuing increasing levels of responsibility as providers, protectors, and connectors in their realm of influence? Are they joyfully building a culture and legacy of love and nourishment in their marriages and relationships with their children? Or are they struggling, discouraged, and in survival mode? Do you see them displaying unhealthy physical or emotional behavior or compulsions? Are their relationships dysfunctional or in shambles? Are they living in isolation? Do they have a "battle buddy"?

As you consider these men, notice the quality of your friendships. Are your friendships focused on helping each other become men of courage and skill in all areas of life, or just on doing things together? When was the last time you had a vulnerable conversation with a man you consider a friend and told him what was really going on in your life, or invited him to do the same with you? When was the last time you invited another man to give you feedback or keep you accountable for an area of growth in your life?

Lastly, look in the mirror. Where are you struggling in life right now? What could change about your situation if you had a godly father or brother walking with you through those difficulties and issues? Could it be that the number-one thing you need is the strength of other men in your life? Also, what strength do you have that you're not sharing with the world? Could it be that the sense of purpose and meaning you're seeking lies in finding other men who need what you carry and pouring into them?

I hope you took a moment to honestly consider these questions and come up with some answers. Now that you've done that: What are you prepared to do? Are you prepared to find twelve men and invite them into a journey of covenant together?

As we see with the examples of David and Jesus, the formation of a band of brothers begins with one man—a man who carries a covenant heart towards other men in his life. Jesus put it like this with His twelve disciples, "You did not choose Me, but I chose you and appointed you that you should go and bear fruit, and that your fruit should remain, that whatever you ask the Father in My name He may give you. These things I command you, that you love one another" (John 15:16-17).

If your answer is yes, then I invite you to follow the steps I laid out above to start:

1. Pray and ask the Lord to show you who belongs in your Twelve.
2. Use the "Billy's Twelve Ingredients" as your criteria.
3. Start slow and build—remember, this is a marathon, not a sprint.
4. Once you have your Twelve on board, integrate the Dragon Slayer creed.
5. Schedule out the year of your monthly meetings (in person, on Zoom or both). The monthly rhythm seems to be good for building connections as a group.
6. Assign "battle buddies" for the men to get to know each other better and check in with each other weekly.
7. Create a twenty-four-month plan for your monthly meetings. Start by getting to know each other. Then I recommend having everyone read *The Way of the Dragon Slayer* and complete the activations on your calls.
8. Plan gatherings of your men during those first two years. Try to include some adventure, "nature danger," or activities that test you emotionally and physically as well as give you the chance to get to know and enjoy each other more.
9. Remember that men bond by doing much more than by talking. So, find things to do like clean up a yard for someone, fix a porch, or get dirty and sweaty helping someone else.

10. Clarify your measures of success as a group. These should major on personal growth in the seven areas of relationship and responsibility in this book, growth of connection between your twelve brothers, and growth in their journey to start gathering and leading twelve men of their own.

Again, this is just the start of what will be a lifelong journey together and with the larger Dragon Slayers tribe and movement of men. This book is the first of many resources, events, and opportunities we will generate to support you on your journey. Stay tuned!

We Will Turn the Tide

There is no doubt in my mind that the solution to the burning village that is our modern society is this: covenant-hearted men choosing other men, walking with them through life, and helping them conquer their dragons of fear and insecurity so they become mature men who can father the next generation. I know this because it's already happened in history. That is the story of the early church and the men who "turned the world upside down" (Acts 17:6). Church history has seen many periods of decline and prodigal generations like ours, but every time the Spirit of our ultimate covenant Friend, Jesus, has come to reawaken our first love, bring us back to the Father, and restore us to our place in the family of God as sons, brothers, husbands, fathers, and leaders.

The truth is that all the problems we're facing today are the fruit of the last four or five decades. It's not hard to trace our current cultural cancers back to landmark decisions and events that happened, for many of us, in our lifetimes or our parents' lifetimes—the separation of church and state, removing prayer from schools, legalized abortion, no-fault divorce, the Sexual Revolution, Playboy magazine, James Bond as a masculine icon, the infiltration of our schools and universities by social radicals, etc. None of those events were caused by mass movements, but by a remarkably small group of people. As Margaret Mead put it, "Never doubt that a small group of thoughtful, committed citizens can change the world; indeed, it's the only thing that ever has." If those people could change the world for the worse, then we can certainly change it for the better over the next forty to fifty years. All we need is to become those "thoughtful, committed" men dedicated to rebuilding everything that has been torn down.

This is why the "small beginnings" I am seeing with Dragon Slayers thrill my heart. This isn't just another avenue for men to get some dopamine hit, adrenaline rush, or emotional high and then go back to business as usual. We are being called into something that is at its root, a move of the Holy Spirit. The DNA of every move of the Spirit follows the declaration of Isaiah 61:1-4, which Jesus read at the start of His ministry. First the Spirit revives and restores His people, freeing the captives, healing the brokenhearted, and consoling those who grieve—and then these liberated, healed, joyful people "rebuild the old ruins, . . . raise up the former desolations, and . . . repair the ruined cities, the desolations of many generations" (Isaiah 61:4).

As someone who has spent my entire Christian life in churches dedicated to the pursuit of revival, I know we tend to focus on things like physical healing and deliverance, prophetic ministry, long worship services, people falling out under the power of God, passionate preaching punctuated with "Amens," and altar calls as the primary signs of the Spirit's activity. I love all of those things, but when Jesus went to the cross, He didn't pray for the Spirit to empower His disciples to have great church meetings. He prayed for us to be one in His love, united as sons and brothers with the same bond He shares with the Father. This is the heart of the Man we follow. This is what His Spirit is working to accomplish in us, and He won't stop until Jesus has what He prayed and paid for in our lives. All we have to do is say yes to Him, and yes to one another. What are you prepared to do?

www.DragonSlayers.co

VISIT THE
DRAGON SLAYERS
WEBSITE

DISCOVER DANNY'S BOOK RECOMMENDATIONS FOR MEN

UNPUNISHABLE
Danny Silk

KEEP YOUR LOVE ON
Danny Silk

POWERFUL & FREE
Danny Silk

IMPERFECT PARENTING
Brittney Serpel

WILD AT HEART
John Eldredge

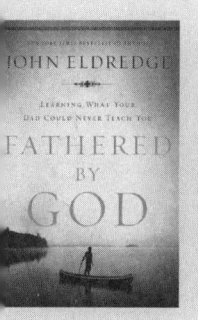

FATHERED BY GOD
John Eldredge

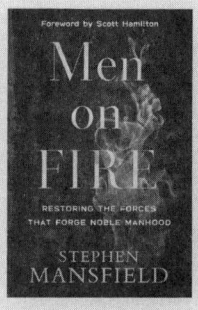

MEN ON FIRE
Stephen Mansfield

MANSFIELD'S BOOK OF MANLY MEN
Stephen Mansfield

BUILDING YOUR BAND OF BROTHERS
Stephen Mansfield

THE MEN WE NEED
Brant Hansen

More Loving on Purpose books at
lovingonpurpose.com/lop-store

LISTEN TO THE LOVING ON PURPOSE PODCAST NETWORK

DRAGON SLAYERS

Discover the Dragon Slayers Podcast, where ordinary men share extraordinary tales of conquering fears and becoming fearless, loving men of God. Gain wisdom, practical advice, and brotherhood, so you can stand out as a man among men. Will you join us?

THE KYLO SHOW

We believe whole, healthy families are going to save the world. So join us as we uncover how to practically keep your love on.

IMPERFECT PARENTING

Ready to infuse hope back into your parenting? Join Brittney and Ben Serpell as they teach how to cultivate a safe, loving, heart-to-heart connection with your kids.

LOVING ON PURPOSE PODCAST NETWORK

Find out more about our podcasts:
lovingonpurpose.com/podcast

DRAGON CHEAT SHEET

Man with God
The fear of punishment, judgment, and unworthiness

Man with Himself
The fear of inadequacy, self-hatred, and disqualification

Man with Women
The fear of rejection, disconnection, and betrayal

Man with Men
The fear of competition, covenant, and sacrifice

Man with Nature
The fear of insignificance, vulnerability, and eternity

Man with Machine
The fear of failure, being out of control, and death

Man with Provision
The fear of lack, limitation, and comparison